797,885 Books

are available to read at

www.ForgottenBooks.com

Forgotten Books' App
Available for mobile, tablet & eReader

ISBN 978-1-331-46409-9
PIBN 10193703

This book is a reproduction of an important historical work. Forgotten Books uses state-of-the-art technology to digitally reconstruct the work, preserving the original format whilst repairing imperfections present in the aged copy. In rare cases, an imperfection in the original, such as a blemish or missing page, may be replicated in our edition. We do, however, repair the vast majority of imperfections successfully; any imperfections that remain are intentionally left to preserve the state of such historical works.

Forgotten Books is a registered trademark of FB &c Ltd.
Copyright © 2017 FB &c Ltd.
FB &c Ltd, Dalton House, 60 Windsor Avenue, London, SW19 2RR.
Company number 08720141. Registered in England and Wales.

For support please visit www.forgottenbooks.com

1 MONTH OF FREE READING

at
www.ForgottenBooks.com

By purchasing this book you are eligible for one month membership to ForgottenBooks.com, giving you unlimited access to our entire collection of over 700,000 titles via our web site and mobile apps.

To claim your free month visit: www.forgottenbooks.com/free193703

* Offer is valid for 45 days from date of purchase. Terms and conditions apply.

English
Français
Deutsche
Italiano
Español
Português

www.forgottenbooks.com

Mythology Photography **Fiction**
Fishing Christianity **Art** Cooking
Essays Buddhism Freemasonry
Medicine **Biology** Music **Ancient Egypt** Evolution Carpentry Physics
Dance Geology **Mathematics** Fitness
Shakespeare **Folklore** Yoga Marketing
Confidence Immortality Biographies
Poetry **Psychology** Witchcraft
Electronics Chemistry History **Law**
Accounting **Philosophy** Anthropology
Alchemy Drama Quantum Mechanics
Atheism Sexual Health **Ancient History**
Entrepreneurship Languages Sport
Paleontology Needlework Islam
Metaphysics Investment Archaeology
Parenting Statistics Criminology
Motivational

MAYNARD'S
English·Classic·Series

GRANDFATHER'S CHAIR

Nathaniel Hawthorne

NEW YORK
MAYNARD, MERRILL & Co.
43, 45 & 47 East 10th St.

ENGLISH CLASSIC SERIES,

FOR

Classes in English Literature, Reading, Grammar, etc

EDITED BY EMINENT ENGLISH AND AMERICAN SCHOLARS.

Each Volume contains a Sketch of the Author's Life, Prefatory and Explanatory Notes, etc., etc.

1 Byron's Prophecy of Dante. (Cantos I. and II.)
2 Milton's L'Allegro, and Il Penseroso.
3 Lord Bacon's Essays, Civil and Moral. (Selected.)
4 Byron's Prisoner of Chillon.
5 Moore's Fire Worshippers. (Lalla Rookh. Selected.)
6 Goldsmith's Deserted Village.
7 Scott's Marmion. (Selections from Canto VI.)
8 Scott's Lay of the Last Minstrel. (Introduction and Canto I.)
9 Burns's Cotter's Saturday Night, and other Poems
10 Crabbe's The Village.
11 Campbell's Pleasures of Hope. (Abridgment of Part I.)
12 Macaulay's Essay on Bunyan's Pilgrim's Progress.
13 Macaulay's Armada, and other Poems.
14 Shakespeare's Merchant of Venice. (Selections from Acts I, III, and IV.)
15 Goldsmith's Traveller.
16 Hogg's Queen's Wake, and Kilmeny.
17 Coleridge's Ancient Mariner.
18 Addison's Sir Roger de Coverley.
19 Gray's Elegy in a Country Churchyard.
20 Scott's Lady of the Lake. (Canto I.)
21 Shakespeare's As You Like It, etc. (Selections.)
22 Shakespeare's King John, and Richard II. (Selections.)
23 Shakespeare's Henry IV., Henry V., Henry VI. (Selections.)
24 Shakespeare's Henry VIII., and Julius Cæsar. (Selections.)
25 Wordsworth's Excursion. (Bk.I.)
26 Pope's Essay on Criticism.
27 Spenser's Faerie Queene. (Cantos I. and II.)
28 Cowper's Task. (Book I.)
29 Milton's Comus.
30 Tennyson's Enoch Arden, The Lotus Eaters, Ulysses, and Tithonus.
31 Irving's Sketch Book. (Selections.)
32 Dickens's Christmas Carol (Condensed.)
33 Carlyle's Hero as a Prophet.
34 Macaulay's Warren Hastings (Condensed.)
35 Goldsmith's Vicar of Wakefield. (Condensed.)
36 Tennyson's The Two Voices and A Dream of Fair Women
37 Memory Quotations.
38 Cavalier Poets.
39 Dryden's Alexander's Feas and MacFlecknoe.
40 Keats's The Eve of St. Agnes.
41 Irving's Legend of Sleepy Hollow.
42 Lamb's Tales from Shakespeare.
43 Le Row's How to Teach Reading.
44 Webster's Bunker Hill Orations.
45 The Academy Orthoëpist. Manual of Pronunciation.
46 Milton's Lycidas, and Hymn on the Nativity.
47 Bryant's Thanatopsis, and other Poems.
48 Ruskin's Modern Painter (Selections)
49 The Shakespeare Speaker.
50 Thackeray's Roundabout Papers.
51 Webster's Oration on Adams and Jefferson.
52 Brown's Rab and his Friends.
53 Morris's Life and Death of Jason.
54 Burke's Speech on America Taxation.
55 Pope's Rape of the Lock.
56 Tennyson's Elaine.
57 Tennyson's In Memoriam.
58 Church's Story of the Æneid.
59 Church's Story of the Iliad.
60 Swift's Gulliver's Voyage Lilliput.
61 Macaulay's Essay on Lord Bacon. (Condensed.)
62 The Alcestis of Euripides. English Version by Rev. R. Potter, M.

(Additional numbers on next page.)

MAYNARD'S ENGLISH CLASSIC SERIES.—No. 184

GRANDFATHER'S CHAIR

PART I

BY

NATHANIEL HAWTHORNE

With Biographical Sketch

NEW YORK
MAYNARD, MERRILL, & CO.

New Series, No. 120. February 23, 1893. Published Semi-weekly. Subscription Price $10. Entered at Post Office, New York, as Second-class Matter.

A Complete Course in the Study of English.

Spelling, Language, Grammar, Composition, Literature.

Reed's Word Lessons—A Complete Speller.
Reed's Introductory Language Work.
Reed & Kellogg's Graded Lessons in English.
Reed & Kellogg's Higher Lessons in English.
Reed & Kellogg's One-Book Course in English.
Kellogg & Reed's Word Building.
Kellogg & Reed's The English Language.
Kellogg's Text-Book on Rhetoric.
Kellogg's Illustrations of Style.
Kellogg's Text-Book on English Literature.

In the preparation of this series the authors have had one object clearly in view—to so develop the study of the English language as to present a complete, progressive course, from the Spelling-Book to the study of English Literature. The troublesome contradictions which arise in using books arranged by different authors on these subjects, and which require much time for explanation in the school-room, will be avoided by the use of the above " Complete Course."

Teachers are earnestly invited to examine these books.

MAYNARD, MERRILL, & CO., PUBLISHERS,

43, 45, and 47 East Tenth St., New York.

Copyright, 1896, by MAYNARD, MERRILL, & Co.

Biographical Sketch

NATHANIEL HAWTHORNE came of a stern, New England ancestry. The founder of the family in this country, William Hathorne (so spelled, but pronounced nearly as afterwards changed by Hawthorne), emigrated from England in 1630, and became a man of some prominence in the new country, a magistrate and deputy in the colonial assembly. His son, Judge John Hawthorne, was prominent in the Salem witchcraft persecutions, and earned an unenviable reputation for harsh judgments. His nature is well shown by the following account of a trial at which he presided.

Of one accused woman brought before him, the husband wrote: "She was forced to stand with her arms stretched out. I requested that I might hold one of her hands, but it was declined me; then she desired me to wipe the tears from her eyes, which I did; then she desired that she might lean herself on me, saying she should faint. Justice Hathorne replied she had strength enough to torture these persons, and she should have strength enough to stand. I repeating something against their cruel proceedings, they commanded me to be silent, or else I should be turned out of the room."

The third son of Judge Hathorne was "Farmer Joseph," who lived and died peaceably at Salem. Joseph's fifth son, "Bold Daniel," became a privateersman in the Revolutionary War. Daniel's third son, Nathaniel, was born in 1775, and was the father of our author.

Hawthorne's father was a sea-captain, reserved, melancholy, and stern, and said to be fond of reading and of children. He married Elizabeth Manning, a descendant of Richard Manning,

BIOGRAPHICAL SKETCH

of Dartmouth, England, and at Salem, Massachusetts, on July 4, 1804, Nathaniel Hawthorne, the author, was born.

His father died four years after, and Hawthorne was brought up by his grandfather Manning, who paid for his education.

In later life Hawthorne wrote that "one of the peculiarities" of his boyhood was "a grievous disinclination to go to school." He appears to have been an adventurous boy, fond of all outdoor exercises, until an accident in playing ball injured his foot. This lameness lasted a long while and restricted his boyish activity so that he took to reading as a pastime. His letters written at this time contain frequent allusions to books, and also occasional scraps of poetry.

In 1821 Hawthorne entered Bowdoin College, where he had the good fortune to be a classmate of Longfellow. Another classmate was Jonathan Cilley, afterwards a member of Congress. Franklin Pierce, afterwards President of the United States and an intimate friend, was at that time a sophomore.

These friendships appear to have been about all that he gained from his college life. "I was an idle student," he wrote in after years, "negligent of college rules and the Procrustean details of academic life, rather choosing to nurse my own fancies than to dig Greek roots and be numbered among the learned Thebans." His extreme shyness is shown by the fact that he regularly paid fines rather than make declamations.

Hawthorne graduated in 1825, and returned to Salem, where he settled in the gloomy old family mansion and began to write; at first tentatively, and later with the avowed purpose of making literature his profession. In his "Note Book," under date of October 4, 1840, he says: "Here I sit in this accustomed chamber where I used to sit in days gone by. . . . Here I have written many tales,—many that have been burned to ashes, many that doubtless deserve the same fate. . . . and here I sat a long, long time, waiting patiently for the world to know me, and sometimes wondering why it did not know me sooner, or whether it would ever know me at all,—at least, till I were in my grave."

He finally published some tales in the magazines, but these hardly served the purpose of bringing him fairly before the public. "It was like a man talking to himself in a dark place," he said.

It was not until March, 1837, that Hawthorne succeeded in getting a volume, the first series of "Twice Told Tales," published. It brought him an excellent review by Longfellow, of which a portion is given in the "Critical Opinions," and brought him before the world of letters as an accredited author; but financially was not fortunate, as the sales barely paid the cost of publication. Before long, however, the young author's necessities were relieved by an appointment to the Boston Custom House as weigher and gauger at a salary of $1,200. This was hardly a congenial occupation for a man of a poetical temperament, but Hawthorne made the best of it, and, at the end of his tenure of office (he was removed by a change of administration) had saved one thousand dollars from his salary.

Carlyle at this time was speaking to the youth of America through Emerson with a voice of thunder, and transcendentalism was abroad in the land. Hawthorne's friends, the Peabodys, were Emersonian enthusiasts, and it was probably through their influence that he was drawn into the Brook Farm community, which seemed to promise an economical retreat, where he could find congenial society and the leisure to write. He embarked his thousand dollars in this enterprise, and arrived at Brook Farm, April 12, 1841. This community was an unconventional society of cultivated men and women, sick of politics, and hoping by a communal existence to release much time for the development of their individual genius.

Hawthorne remained in the community about a year. But before he left he had made the discovery that he had never been really there in heart. "The real Me was never an associate of the community; there has been a spectral Appearance there, sounding the horn at daybreak, and milking the cows, and hoeing potatoes, and raking hay, toiling in the sun, and doing me the honor to assume my name. But this spectre was not myself." But the great eye of Hawthorne was there, and every scene was pictured on it. It was the sufficient *raison d'être* of Brook Farm that it produced that truly American novel "The Blithedale Romance."

Hawthorne was married in 1842, and went to live at "The Old Manse" at Concord, Massachusetts. Here he spent four happy years, enjoying the society of Emerson, Thoreau, Ellery Channing,—who, Emerson said, wrote "poetry for poets"—and of other cultivated men and women.

In 1846 Hawthorne was appointed Surveyor of Customs at Salem, Massachusetts. He held this position until 1849, but, as the office must have been irksome to him, and the Salem people did not treat him with any geniality, he was probably not sorry when a change of administration ousted him from his position.

Once more he settled down to steady literary work, with the result that in 1850 "The Scarlet Letter" appeared, and achieved such a marked success that he was enabled to remove to Lenox, Massachusetts. His next book was "The House of Seven Gables." In 1851 he removed to West Newton, Massachusetts, where "The Blithedale Romance" was written, and in 1852 he moved again to Concord.

In 1853 Hawthorne was appointed United States Consul to Liverpool, and for six years nothing appeared from his pen. His stay in England seems to have been a failure. He met none of the great men of letters, then so numerous in England, except the Brownings. He never really liked the English, and after they had read his "Our Old Home," they very generally felt the same toward him. It is in this volume that he describes Englishwomen as made up of steaks and sirloins, a remark which not unnaturally stirred up a strong feeling of resentment in England.

After leaving Liverpool in 1857, Hawthorne and his family travelled south, and in January, 1858, they settled in Rome. Except for the illness of his eldest daughter, the next two years were among the happiest of Hawthorne's life. He enjoyed the society he met in Rome; W. W. Story the eminent sculptor, the historian Motley, William Cullen Bryant, Mrs.

Jameson and other cultivated people being his intimates. He had come to Rome, however, merely as a pleasant excursion, having little or no knowledge of art, and no taste for ruins, so that it was some time before he began to take Rome seriously. The stay bore fruit when he returned to England on his way back to America, in the form of "The Marble Faun," probably his most popular book.

In 1860 Hawthorne settled again in Concord with the intention of giving himself up to his literary work, but it was not to be for long. Presently the war broke out, and he became gloomy and unable to work, and in 1864 he died when on a trip to New Hampshire with his old friend, Franklin Pierce. He was buried at Concord, on May 24, 1864.

This slight sketch may fitly close by a description of Hawthorne's personal appearance by his friend and biographer, Moncure D. Conway.

"He impressed me—the present writer—as of much nobler presence than formerly, and certainly he was one of the finest-looking of men. I observed him closely at a dinner of the Literary Club, in Boston, the great feature of which was the presence of Hawthorne, then just from Europe (July, 1860). His great athletic frame was softened by its repose, which was the more striking beside the vivacity of Agassiz, at whose side he sat—himself a magnificent man in appearance. Hawthorne's massive brow and fine aquiline nose were of such commanding strength as to make the mouth and chin seem a little weak by contrast. The upper lip was hidden by a thick moustache; the under lip was somewhat too pronounced, perhaps. The head was most shapely in front, but at the back was singularly flat. This peculiarity appears in a bust of Hawthorne now in possession of his friend and banker, Mr. Hooker, at Rome. It is by Phillips, and is especially interesting as representing the author in early life, before the somewhat severe mouth was modified by a moustache. The eyes were at once dark and lucid, very large but never staring, incurious, soft and pathetic as those of a deer. When addressed, a gracious smile accompanied his always gentle reply, and the most engaging expression suffused his warm brown face. The smile, however, was sweet only while in the eyes; when it extended to the mouth it seemed to give him pain. There must have been battles between those soft eyes and this mouth. His voice was sweet and low, but suggested a reserve of quick and powerful intelligence. In conversation, the trait that struck me most was his perfect candor. There was no faintest suggestion of secrecy. I have a suspicion that his shyness was that of one whose heart was without bolts or bars, and who felt himself at the mercy of every 'interviewer' that might chance to get hold of him."

PREFACE

In writing this ponderous tome, the author's desire has been to describe the eminent characters and remarkable events of our early annals in such a form and style that the YOUNG might make acquaintance with them of their own accord. For this purpose, while ostensibly relating the adventures of a chair, he has endeavored to keep a distinct and unbroken thread of authentic history. The chair is made to pass from one to another of those personages of whom he thought it most desirable for the young reader to have vivid and familiar ideas, and whose lives and actions would best enable him to give picturesque sketches of the times.

There is certainly no method by which the shadowy outlines of departed men and women can be made to assume the hues of life more effectually than by connecting their images with the substantial and homely reality of a fireside chair. It causes us to feel at once that these characters of history had a private and familiar existence, and were not wholly contained within that cold array of outward action which we are compelled to receive as the adequate representation of their lives. If this impression can be given, much is accomplished.

Setting aside Grandfather and his auditors, and excepting the adventures of the chair, which form the machinery of the work, nothing in the ensuing pages can be termed fictitious. The author, it is true, has sometimes assumed the license of filling up the outline of history with details for which he has none but imaginative authority, but which, he hopes, do not violate nor give a false coloring to the truth. He believes that, in this respect, his narrative will not be found to convey ideas and impressions of which the reader may hereafter find it necessary to purge his mind.

The author's great doubt is, whether he has succeeded in writing a book which will be readable by the class for whom he intends it. To make a lively and entertaining narrative for children, with such unmalleable material as is presented by the sober, stern, and rigid characteristics of the Puritans and their descendants, is quite as difficult an attempt as to manufacture delicate playthings out of the granite rocks on which New England is founded.

BOSTON, November, 1840.

GRANDFATHER'S CHAIR

PART I

CHAPTER I

GRANDFATHER had been sitting in his old armchair all that pleasant afternoon, while the children were pursuing their various sports far off or near at hand. Sometimes you would have said, "Grandfather is asleep"; but still, even when his eyes were closed, his thoughts were with the young people, playing among the flowers and shrubbery of the garden.

He heard the voice of Laurence, who had taken possession of a heap of decayed branches which the gardener had lopped from the fruit trees, and was building a little hut for his cousin Clara and himself. He heard Clara's gladsome voice, too, as she weeded and watered the flower-bed which had been given her for her own. He could have counted every footstep that Charley took, as he trundled his wheelbarrow along the gravel walk. And though

Grandfather was old and gray-haired, yet his heart leaped with joy whenever little Alice came fluttering, like a butterfly, into the room. She had made each of the children her playmate in turn, and now made Grandfather her playmate too, and thought him the merriest of them all.

At last the children grew weary of their sports; because a summer afternoon is like a long lifetime to the young. So they came into the room together, and clustered round Grandfather's great chair. Little Alice, who was hardly five years old, took the privilege of the youngest, and climbed his knee. It was a pleasant thing to behold that fair and golden-haired child in the lap of the old man, and to think that, different as they were, the hearts of both could be gladdened with the same joys.

"Grandfather," said little Alice, laying her head back upon his arm, "I am very tired now. You must tell me a story to make me go to sleep."

"That is not what story-tellers like," answered Grandfather, smiling. "They are better satisfied when they can keep their auditors awake."

"But here are Laurence, and Charley, and I," cried cousin Clara, who was twice as old as little Alice. "We will all three keep wide awake. And pray, Grandfather, tell us a story about this strange-looking old chair."

Now, the chair in which Grandfather sat was

made of oak, which had grown dark with age, but had been rubbed and polished till it shone as bright as mahogany. It was very large and heavy, and had a back that rose high above Grandfather's white head. This back was curiously carved in open-work, so as to represent flowers, and foliage, and other devices, which the children had often gazed at, but could never understand what they meant. On the very tip-top of the chair, over the head of Grandfather himself, was a likeness of a lion's head, which had such a savage grin that you would almost expect to hear it growl and snarl.

The children had seen Grandfather sitting in this chair ever since they could remember anything. Perhaps the younger of them supposed that he and the chair had come into the world together, and that both had always been as old as they were now. At this time, however, it happened to be the fashion for ladies to adorn their drawing rooms with the oldest and oddest chairs that could be found. It seemed to cousin Clara that, if these ladies could have seen Grandfather's old chair, they would have thought it worth all the rest together. She wondered if it were not even older than Grandfather himself, and longed to know all about its history.

"Do, Grandfather, talk to us about this chair," she repeated.

"Well, child," said Grandfather, patting

Clara's cheek, "I can tell you a great many stories of my chair. Perhaps your cousin Laurence would like to hear them, too. They will teach him something about the history and distinguished people of his country which he has never read in any of his schoolbooks."

Cousin Laurence was a boy of twelve, a bright scholar, in whom an early thoughtfulness and sensibility began to show themselves. His young fancy kindled at the idea of knowing all the adventures of this venerable chair. He looked eagerly in Grandfather's face; and even Charley, a bold, brisk, restless little fellow of nine, sat himself down on the carpet, and resolved to be quiet for at least ten minutes, should the story last so long.

Meantime, little Alice was already asleep; so Grandfather, being much pleased with such an attentive audience, began to talk about matters that had happened long ago.

CHAPTER II

BUT before relating the adventures of the chair, Grandfather found it necessary to speak of the circumstances that caused the first settlement of New England. For it will soon be perceived that the story of this remarkable chair cannot be told without telling a good deal of the history of the country.

So Grandfather talked about the Puritans, as those persons were called who thought it sinful to practice the religious forms and ceremonies which the Church of England had borrowed from the Roman Catholics. These Puritans suffered so much persecution in England that, in 1607, many of them went over to Holland, and lived ten or twelve years at Amsterdam and Leyden. But they feared that, if they continued there much longer, they should cease to be English, and should adopt all the manners, and ideas, and feelings of the Dutch. For this and other reasons, in the year 1620 they embarked on board of the ship *Mayflower*, and crossed the ocean to the shores of Cape Cod. There they made a settlement, and called it Plymouth, which, though now a part of Massachusetts, was for a long time a colony by itself. And thus was formed the earliest settlement of the Puritans in America.

Meantime, those of the Puritans who remained in England continued to suffer grievous persecutions on account of their religious opinions. They began to look around them for some spot where they might worship God, not as the king and bishops thought fit, but according to the dictates of their own consciences. When their brethren had gone from Holland to America, they bethought themselves that they likewise might find refuge from persecution there. Several gentlemen among them purchased a tract of country on the coast of Massachusetts Bay, and obtained a charter from King Charles, which authorized them to make laws for the settlers. In the year 1628 they sent over a few people, with John Endicott at their head, to commence a plantation at Salem. Peter Palfrey, Roger Conant, and one or two more had built houses there in 1626, and may be considered as the first settlers of that ancient town. Many other Puritans prepared to follow Endicott.

"And now we come to the chair, my dear children," said Grandfather. "This chair is supposed to have been made of an oak tree which grew in the park of the English Earl of Lincoln between two and three centuries ago. In its younger days it used, probably, to stand in the hall of the earl's castle. Do not you see the coat of arms of the family of Lincoln carved in the open-work of the back? But when his daughter, the Lady Arbella, was married to a certain Mr. Johnson, the earl gave her this valuable chair."

"Who was Mr. Johnson?" inquired Clara.

"He was a gentleman of great wealth, who agreed with the Puritans in their religious opinions," answered Grandfather. "And as his belief was the same as theirs, he resolved that he would live and die with them. Accordingly, in the month of April, 1630, he left his pleasant abode and all his comforts in England, and embarked, with Lady Arbella, on board of a ship bound for America."

As Grandfather was frequently impeded by the questions and observations of his young auditors, we deem it advisable to omit all such prattle as is not essential to the story. We have taken some pains to find out exactly what Grandfather said, and here offer to our readers, as nearly as possible in his own words, the story of

THE LADY ARBELLA

The ship in which Mr. Johnson and his lady embarked, taking Grandfather's chair along with them, was called the *Arbella*, in honor of the lady herself. A fleet of ten or twelve vessels, with many hundred passengers, left England about the same time; for a multitude of people, who were discontented with the king's government and oppressed by the bishops, were flocking over to the New World. One of the vessels in the fleet was that same *Mayflower* which had carried the Puritan pilgrims to Plymouth. And now, my children, I would have you fancy yourselves in the cabin of the good ship *Arbella*; because if you could behold the passengers aboard that vessel, you would feel what a blessing and honor it was for New England to have such settlers. They were the best men and women of their day.

Among the passengers was John Winthrop, who had sold the estate of his forefathers, and was going to prepare a new home for his wife and children in the wilderness. He had the king's charter in his keeping, and was appointed the first Governor of Massachusetts. Imagine him a person of grave and benevolent aspect, dressed in a black velvet suit, with a broad ruff around his neck, and a peaked beard upon his chin. There was likewise a minister of the gospel whom the English bishops had forbidden to preach, but who knew that he should have liberty both to preach and pray in the forests of America. He wore a black cloak, called a Geneva cloak, and had a black velvet cap, fitting close to his head, as was the fashion of almost all the Puritan clergymen. In their company came Sir Richard Saltonstall, who had been one of the five first projectors of the new colony. He soon returned to his native country. But his descendants still remain in New England; and the good old family name is as much respected in our days as it was in those of Sir Richard.

Not only these, but several other men of wealth and pious ministers were in the cabin of the *Arbella*. One had banished himself forever from the old hall where his ancestors had lived for hundreds of years. Another had left his quiet parsonage, in a country town of England. Others had come from the universities of Oxford or Cambridge, where they had gained great fame for their learning. And here they all were, tossing upon the uncertain and dangerous sea, and bound for a home that was more dangerous than even the sea itself. In the cabin, likewise, sat the Lady Arbella in her chair, with a gentle and sweet expression on her face, but looking too pale and feeble to endure the hardships of the wilderness.

Every morning and evening the Lady Arbella gave up her great chair to one of the ministers, who took his place in it and read passages from the Bible to his companions. And thus, with prayers, and pious conversation, and frequent singing of hymns, which the breezes caught from their lips and scattered far over the desolate waves, they prosecuted their voyage, and sailed into the harbor of Salem in the month of June.

At that period there were but six or eight dwellings in the town; and these were miserable hovels, with roofs of straw and wooden chimneys. The passengers in the fleet either built huts with bark and branches of trees, or erected tents of cloth till they could provide themselves with better shelter. Many of them went to form a settlement at Charlestown. It was thought fit that the Lady Arbella should tarry in Salem for a time: she was probably received as a guest into the family of John Endicott. He was the chief person in the plantation, and had the only comfortable house which the new-comers had beheld since they left England. So now, children, you must imagine Grandfather's chair in the midst of a new scene.

Suppose it a hot summer's day, and the lattice windows of a chamber in Mr. Endicott's house thrown wide open. The Lady Arbella, looking paler than she did on shipboard, is sitting in her chair and thinking mournfully of far-off England. She rises and goes to the window. There, amid patches of garden ground and cornfield, she sees the few wretched hovels of the settlers, with the still ruder wigwams and cloth tents of the passengers who had arrived in the same fleet with herself. Far and near stretches the dismal forest of pine trees, which throw their black shadows over the whole land, and likewise over the heart of this poor lady.

All the inhabitants of the little village are busy. One is clearing a spot on the verge of the forest for his homestead: another is hewing the trunk of a fallen pine tree, in order to build himself a dwelling; a third is hoeing in his field of Indian corn. Here comes a huntsman out of the woods, dragging a bear which he has shot, and shouting to the neighbors to lend him a hand. There goes a man to the seashore, with a spade and a bucket, to dig a mess of clams, which were a principal article of food with the first settlers. Scattered here and there are two or three dusky figures, clad in mantles of fur, with ornaments of bone hanging from their ears, and the feathers of wild birds in their coal-black hair. They have belts of shell-work slung across their shoulders, and are armed with bows and arrows and flint-headed spears. These are an Indian Sagamore and his attendants, who have come to gaze at the labors of the white men. And now rises a cry that a pack of wolves have seized a young calf in the pasture; and every man snatches up his gun or pike and runs in chase of the marauding beasts.

Poor Lady Arbella watches all these sights, and feels that this New World is fit only for rough and hardy people. None should be here but those who can struggle with wild beasts and wild men, and can toil in the heat or cold, and can keep their hearts firm against all difficulties and dangers. But she is not one of these. Her gentle and timid spirit sinks within her; and, turning away from the window, she sits down in the great chair and wonders whereabouts in the wilderness her friends will dig her grave.

Mr. Johnson had gone, with Governor Winthrop and most of the other passengers, to Boston, where he intended to build a house for Lady Arbella and himself. Boston was then covered with wild woods, and had fewer inhabitants, even, than Salem. During her husband's absence, poor Lady Arbella felt herself growing ill, and was hardly able to stir from the great chair. Whenever John Endicott noticed her despondency, he doubtless addressed her with words of comfort. "Cheer up, my good lady!" he would say. "In a little time, you will love this rude life of the wilderness as I do." But Endicott's heart was as bold and resolute as iron, and he could not understand why a woman's heart should not be of iron too.

Still, however, he spoke kindly to the lady, and then hastened forth to till his cornfield and set out fruit trees, or to bargain with the Indians for furs, or perchance to oversee the building of a fort. Also, being a magistrate, he had often to punish some idler or evil doer, by ordering him to be set in the stocks or scourged at the whipping-post. Often, too, as was the custom of the times, he and Mr. Higginson, the minister of Salem, held long religious talks together. Thus John Endicott was a man of multifarious business, and had no time to look back regretfully to his native land. He felt himself fit for the New World and for the work that he had to do, and set himself resolutely to accomplish it.

What a contrast, my dear children, between this bold, rough, active man, and the gentle Lady Arbella, who was fading away, like a pale

English flower, in the shadow of the forest! And now the great chair was often empty, because Lady Arbella grew too weak to arise from bed.

Meantime, her husband had pitched upon a spot for their new home. He returned from Boston to Salem, traveling through the woods on foot, and leaning on his pilgrim's staff. His heart yearned within him; for he was eager to tell his wife of the new home which he had chosen. But when he beheld her pale and hollow cheek, and found how her strength was wasted, he must have known that her appointed home was in a better land. Happy for him then —happy both for him and her—if they remembered that there was a path to heaven, as well from this heathen wilderness as from the Christian land whence they had come. And so, in one short month from her arrival, the gentle Lady Arbella faded away and died. They dug a grave for her in the new soil, where the roots of the pine trees impeded their spades; and when her bones had rested there nearly two hundred years, and a city had sprung up around them, a church of stone was built upon the spot.

Charley, almost at the commencement of the foregoing narrative, had galloped away, with a prodigious clatter, upon Grandfather's stick, and was not yet returned. So large a boy should have been ashamed to ride upon a stick. But Laurence and Clara had listened attentively, and were affected by this true story of the gentle lady who had come so far to die so soon. Grandfather had supposed that little Alice was asleep; but toward the close of the story, happening to look down upon her, he saw that her blue eyes were wide open, and fixed earnestly upon his face. The tears had gathered in them, like dew upon a delicate flower; but when Grandfather ceased to speak, the sunshine of her smile broke forth again.

"Oh, the lady must have been so glad to get to heaven!" exclaimed little Alice.

"Grandfather, what became of Mr. Johnson?" asked Clara.

"His heart appears to have been quite broken," answered Grandfather; "for he died at Boston within a month after the death of his wife. He was buried in the very same tract of ground where he had intended to build a dwelling for Lady Arbella and himself. Where their house would have stood, there was his grave."

"I never heard anything so melancholy," said Clara.

"The people loved and respected Mr. Johnson so much," continued Grandfather, "that it was the last request of many of them, when they died, that they might be buried as near as possible to this good man's grave. And so the field became the first burial-ground in Boston. When you pass through Tremont Street, along by King's Chapel, you see a burial-ground, containing many old gravestones and monuments. That was Mr. Johnson's field."

"How sad is the thought," observed Clara, "that one of the first things which the settlers had to do, when they came to the New World, was to set apart a burial-ground!"

"Perhaps," said Laurence, "if they had found no need of burial-grounds here, they would have been glad, after a few years, to go back to England."

Grandfather looked at Laurence, to discover whether he knew how profound and true a thing he had said.

CHAPTER III

Not long after Grandfather had told the story of his great chair, there chanced to be a rainy day. Our friend Charley, after disturbing the household with beat of drum and riotous shouts, races up and down the staircase, overturning of chairs, and much other uproar, began to feel the quiet and confinement within doors intolerable. But as the rain came down in a flood the little fellow was hopelessly a prisoner, and now stood with sullen aspect at the window, wondering whether the sun itself were not extinguished by so much moisture in the sky.

Charley had already exhausted the less eager activity of the other children; and they had betaken themselves to occupations that did not admit of his companionship. Laurence sat in a recess near the bookcase, reading, not for the first time, the "Midsummer Night's Dream." Clara was making a rosary of beads for a little figure of a Sister of Charity, who was to attend the Bunker Hill fair and lend her aid in erecting the monument. Little Alice sat on Grandfather's footstool, with a picture book in her hand; and, for every picture, the child was telling Grandfather a story. She did not read from the book (for little Alice had not much skill in reading), but told the story out of her own heart and mind.

Charley was too big a boy, of course, to care anything about little Alice's stories, although Grandfather appeared to listen with a good deal of interest. Often, in a young child's ideas and fancies, there is something which it requires the thought of a lifetime to comprehend. But Charley was of opinion that, if a story must be told, it had better be told by Grandfather than little Alice.

"Grandfather, I want to hear more about your chair," said he.

Now, Grandfather remembered that Charley had galloped away upon a stick in the midst of the narrative of poor Lady Arbella, and I know not whether he would have thought it worth while to tell another story merely to gratify such an inattentive auditor as Charley. But Laurence laid down his book and seconded the request. Clara drew her chair nearer to Grandfather; and little Alice immediately closed her picture book and looked up into his face. Grandfather had not the heart to disappoint them.

He mentioned several persons who had a share in the settlement of our country, and who would be well worthy of remembrance, if we could find room to tell about them all. Among the rest, Grandfather spoke of the famous Hugh Peters, a minister of the gospel, who did much good to the inhabitants of Salem. Mr. Peters afterward went back to England, and was chaplain to Oliver Cromwell; but Grandfather did not tell the children what became of this upright and zealous man at last. In fact, his auditors were growing impatient to hear more about the history of the chair.

"After the death of Mr. Johnson," said he, "Grandfather's chair came into the possession of Roger Williams. He was a clergyman, who arrived at Salem, and settled there, in 1631. Doubtless the good man has spent many a studious hour in this old chair, either penning a sermon or reading some abstruse book of theology, till midnight came upon him unawares. At that period, as there were few lamps or candles to be had, people used to read or work by the light of pitch-pine torches. These supplied the place of the 'midnight oil' to the learned men of New England."

Grandfather went on to talk about Roger Williams, and told the children several particulars, which we have not room to repeat. One incident, however, which was connected with his life, must be related, because it will give the reader an idea of the opinions and feelings of the first settlers of New England. It was as follows:

THE RED CROSS

While Roger Williams sat in Grandfather's chair at his humble residence in Salem, John Endicott would often come to visit him. As the clergy had great influence in temporal concerns, the minister and magistrate would talk over the occurrences of the day, and consult how the people might be governed according to scriptural laws.

One thing especially troubled them both. In the old national banner of England, under which her soldiers have fought for hundreds of years, there is a Red Cross, which has been there ever since the days when England was in subjection to the Pope. The Cross, though a holy symbol, was abhorred by the Puritans, because they considered it a relic of popish idolatry. Now, whenever the train-band of Salem was mustered, the soldiers, with Endicott at their head, had no other flag to march under than this same old papistical banner of England, with the Red Cross in the midst of it. The banner of the Red Cross, likewise, was flying on the walls of the fort of Salem; and a similar one was displayed in Boston harbor, from the fortress on Castle Island.

"I profess, Brother Williams," Captain Endicott would say, after they had been talking of this matter, "it distresses a Christian man's heart to see this idolatrous Cross flying over our heads. A stranger, beholding it, would think that we had undergone all our hardships and dangers, by sea and in the wilderness, only to get new dominions for the Pope of Rome."

"Truly, good Mr. Endicott," Roger Williams would answer, "you speak as an honest man and Protestant Christian should. For mine own part, were it my business to draw a sword, I should reckon it sinful to fight under such a banner. Neither can I, in my pulpit, ask the blessing of Heaven upon it."

Such, probably, was the way in which Roger Williams and John Endicott used to talk about the banner of the Red Cross. Endicott, who was a prompt and resolute man, soon determined that Massachusetts, if she could not have a banner of her own, should at least be delivered from that of the Pope of Rome.

Not long afterward there was a military muster at Salem. Every able-bodied man in the town and neighborhood was there. All were well armed, with steel caps upon their heads, plates of iron upon their breasts and at their backs, and gorgets of steel around their necks. When the sun shone upon these ranks of iron-clad men, they flashed and blazed with a splendor that bedazzled the wild Indians who had come out of the woods to gaze at them. The soldiers had long pikes, swords, and muskets, which were fired with matches, and were almost as heavy as a small cannon.

These men had mostly a stern and rigid aspect. To judge by their looks, you might have supposed that there was as much iron in their hearts as there was upon their heads and breasts. They were all devoted Puritans, and of the same temper as those with whom Oliver Cromwell afterward overthrew the throne of England. They hated all the relics of popish superstition as much as Endicott himself; and yet over their heads was displayed the banner of the Red Cross.

Endicott was the captain of the company.

While the soldiers were expecting his orders to begin their exercise, they saw him take the banner in one hand, holding his drawn sword in the other. Probably he addressed them in a speech, and explained how horrible a thing it was that men, who had fled from popish idolatry into the wilderness, should be compelled to fight under its symbols here. Perhaps he concluded his address somewhat in the following style:

"And now, fellow soldiers, you see this old banner of England. Some of you, I doubt not, may think it treason for a man to lay violent hands upon it. But whether or no it be treason to man, I have good assurance in my conscience that it is no treason to God. Wherefore, I have resolved that we will rather be God's soldiers than soldiers of the Pope of Rome; and in that mind I now cut the Papal Cross out of this banner."

And so he did. And thus, in a province belonging to the crown of England, a captain was found bold enough to deface the king's banner with his sword.

When Winthrop and the other wise men of Massachusetts heard of it they were disquieted, being afraid that Endicott's act would bring great trouble upon himself and them. An account of the matter was carried to King Charles; but he was then so much engrossed by dissensions with his people that he had no leisure to punish the offender. In other times, it might have cost Endicott his life and Massachusetts her charter.

"I should like to know, Grandfather," said Laurence, when the story was ended, "whether, when Endicott cut the Red Cross out of the banner, he meant to imply that Massachusetts was independent of England?"

"A sense of the independence of his adopted country must have been in that bold man's heart," answered Grandfather; "but I doubt whether he had given the matter much consideration except in its religious bearing. However, it was a very remarkable affair, and a very strong expression of Puritan character."

Grandfather proceeded to speak further of Roger Williams, and of other persons who sat in the great chair, as will be seen in the following chapter.

CHAPTER IV

"ROGER WILLIAMS," said Grandfather, "did not keep possession of the chair a great while. His opinions of civil and religious matters differed, in many respects, from those of the rulers and clergymen of Massachusetts. Now, the wise men of those days believed that the country could not be safe unless all the inhabitants felt and thought alike."

"Does anybody believe so in our days, Grandfather?" asked Laurence.

"Possibly there are some who believe it," said Grandfather; "but they have not so much power to act upon their belief as the magistrates and ministers had in the days of Roger Williams. They had the power to deprive this good man of his home, and to send him out from the midst of them in search of a new place of rest. He was banished in 1634, and went first to Plymouth colony; but as the people there held the same opinions as those of Massachusetts, he was not suffered to remain among them. However, the wilderness was wide enough; so Roger Williams took his staff and traveled into the forest and made treaties with the Indians, and began a plantation which he called Providence."

"I have been to Providence on the railroad," said Charley. "It is but a two hours' ride."

"Yes, Charley," replied Grandfather; "but when Roger Williams traveled thither, over hills and valleys, and through the tangled woods, and across swamps and streams, it was a journey of several days. Well, his little plantation is now grown to be a populous city; and the inhabitants have a great veneration for Roger Williams. His name is familiar in the mouths of all, because they see it on their bank-bills. How it would have perplexed this good clergyman if he had been told that he should give his name to the ROGER WILLIAMS BANK!"

"When he was driven from Massachusetts," said Laurence, "and began his journey into the woods, he must have felt as if he were burying himself forever from the sight and knowledge of men. Yet the whole country has now heard of him, and will remember him forever."

"Yes," answered Grandfather; "it often happens that the outcasts of one generation are those who are reverenced as the wisest and best of men by the next. The securest fame is that which comes after a man's death. But let us return to our story. When Roger Williams was banished, he appears to have given the chair to Mrs. Anne Hutchinson. At all events, it was in her possession in 1637. She was a very sharp-witted and well-instructed lady, and was so conscious of her own wisdom and abilities that she thought it a pity that the world should not have the benefit of them. She therefore used to hold lectures in Boston once or twice a week, at which most of the women attended. Mrs. Hutchinson presided at these meetings, sitting with great state and dignity in Grandfather's chair."

"Grandfather, was it positively this very chair?" demanded Clara, laying her hand upon its carved elbow.

"Why not, my dear Clara?" said Grandfather. "Well, Mrs. Hutchinson's lectures soon caused a great disturbance; for the ministers of Boston did not think it safe and proper that a woman should publicly instruct the people in religious doctrines. Moreover, she made the matter worse by declaring that the Rev. Mr. Cotton was the only sincerely pious and holy clergyman in New England. Now, the clergy of those days had quite as much share in the government of the country, though indirectly, as the magistrates themselves; so you may imagine what a host of powerful enemies were raised up against Mrs. Hutchinson. A synod was convened; that is to say, an assemblage of all the ministers in Massachusetts. They declared that there were eighty-two erroneous opinions on religious subjects diffused among the people, and that Mrs. Hutchinson's opinions were of the number."

"If they had eighty-two wrong opinions," observed Charley, "I don't see how they could have any right ones."

"Mrs. Hutchinson had many zealous friends and converts," continued Grandfather. "She was favored by young Henry Vane, who had come over from England a year or two before, and had since been chosen Governor of the colony, at the age of twenty-four. But Winthrop and most of the other leading men, as well as the ministers, felt an abhorrence of her doctrines. Thus two opposite parties were formed; and so fierce were the dissensions that it was feared the consequence would be civil war and bloodshed. But Winthrop and the ministers being the most powerful, they disarmed and imprisoned Mrs. Hutchinson's adherents. She, like Roger Williams, was banished."

"Dear Grandfather, did they drive the poor woman into the woods?" exclaimed little Alice, who contrived to feel a human interest even in these discords of polemic divinity.

"They did, my darling," replied Grandfather; "and the end of her life was so sad you must not hear it. At her departure, it appears, from the best authorities, that she gave the great chair to her friend Henry Vane. He was a young man of wonderful talents and great learning, who had imbibed the religious opinions of the Puritans, and left England with the intention of spending his life in Massachusetts. The people chose him Governor; but the controversy about Mrs. Hutchinson, and other troubles, caused him to leave the country in 1637. You may read the subsequent events of his life in the history of England."

"Yes, Grandfather," cried Laurence; "and we may read them better in Mr. Upham's biography of Vane. And what a beautiful death he died, long afterward! Beautiful, though it was on a scaffold."

"Many of the most beautiful deaths have been

there," said Grandfather. "The enemies of a great and good man can in no other way make him so glorious as by giving him the crown of martyrdom."

In order that the children might fully understand the all-important history of the chair, Grandfather now saw fit to speak of the progress that was made in settling several colonies. The settlement of Plymouth, in 1620, has already been mentioned. In 1635 Mr. Hooker and Mr. Stone, two ministers, went on foot from Massachusetts to Connecticut, through the pathless woods, taking their whole congregation along with them. They founded the town of Hartford. In 1638 Mr. Davenport, a very celebrated minister, went with other people, and began a plantation at New Haven. In the same year, some persons who had been persecuted in Massachusetts went to the Isle of Rhodes, since called Rhode Island, and settled there. About this time, also, many settlers had gone to Maine, and were living without any regular government. There were likewise settlers near Piscataqua River, in the region which is now called New Hampshire.

Thus, at various points along the coast of New England, there were communities of Englishmen. Though these communities were independent of one another, yet they had a common dependence upon England; and, at so vast a distance from their native home, the inhabitants must all have felt like brethren. They were fitted to become one united people at a future period. Perhaps their feelings of brotherhood were the stronger because different nations had formed settlements to the north and to the south. In Canada and Nova Scotia were colonies of French. On the banks of the Hudson River was a colony of Dutch, who had taken possession of that region many years before, and called it New Netherlands.

Grandfather, for aught I know, might have gone on to speak of Maryland and Virginia; for the good old gentleman really seemed to suppose that the whole surface of the United States was not too broad a foundation to place the four legs of his chair upon. But, happening to glance at Charley, he perceived that this naughty boy was growing impatient and meditating another ride upon a stick. So here, for the present, Grandfather suspended the history of his chair.

CHAPTER V

THE children had now learned to look upon the chair with an interest which was almost the same as if it were a conscious being, and could remember the many famous people whom it had held within its arms.

Even Charley, lawless as he was, seemed to feel that this venerable chair must not be clambered upon nor overturned, although he had no scruple in taking such liberties with every other chair in the house. Clara treated it with still greater reverence; often taking occasion to smooth its cushion, and to brush the dust from the carved flowers and grotesque figures of its oaken back and arms. Laurence would sometimes sit a whole hour, especially at twilight, gazing at the chair, and, by the spell of his imaginations, summoning up its ancient occupants to appear in it again.

Little Alice evidently employed herself in a similar way, for once when Grandfather had gone abroad, the child was heard talking with the gentle Lady Arbella, as if she were still sitting in the chair. So sweet a child as little Alice may fitly talk with angels, such as the Lady Arbella had long since become.

Grandfather was soon importuned for more stories about the chair. He had no difficulty in relating them; for it really seemed as if every person noted in our early history had, on some occasion or other, found repose within its comfortable arms. If Grandfather took pride in anything, it was in being the possessor of such an honorable and historic elbow chair.

"I know not precisely who next got possession of the chair after Governor Vane went back to England," said Grandfather. "But there is reason to believe that President Dunster sat in it, when he held the first Commencement at Harvard College. You have often heard, children, how careful our forefathers were to give their young people a good education. They had scarcely cut down trees enough to make room for their own dwellings before they began to think of establishing a college. Their principal object was, to rear up pious and learned ministers; and hence old writers call Harvard College a school of the prophets."

"Is the college a school of the prophets now?" asked Charley.

"It is a long while since I took my degree, Charley. You must ask some of the recent graduates," answered Grandfather. "As I was telling you, President Dunster sat in Grandfather's chair in 1642, when he conferred the degree of Bachelor of Arts on nine young men. They were the first in America who had received that honor. And now, my dear auditors, I must confess that there are contradictory statements and some uncertainty about the adventures of the chair for a period of almost ten years. Some say that it was occupied by your own ancestor, William Hawthorne, first Speaker of the House of Representatives. I have nearly satisfied myself, however, that, during most of this questionable period, it was literally the Chair of State.

It gives me much pleasure to imagine that several successive Governors of Massachusetts sat in it at the council board."

"But, Grandfather," interposed Charley, who was a matter-of-fact little person, "what reason have you to imagine so?"

"Pray do imagine it, Grandfather," said Laurence.

"With Charley's permission, I will," replied Grandfather, smiling. "Let us consider it settled, therefore, that Winthrop, Bellingham, Dudley, and Endicott, each of them, when chosen Governor, took his seat in our great chair on election day. In this chair, likewise, did those excellent Governors preside while holding consultations with the chief counselors of the province, who were styled assistants. The Governor sat in this chair, too, whenever messages were brought to him from the Chamber of Representatives."

And here Grandfather took occasion to talk rather tediously about the nature and forms of government that established themselves, almost spontaneously, in Massachusetts and the other New England colonies. Democracies were the natural growth of the New World. As to Massachusetts, it was at first intended that the colony should be governed by a council in London. But in a little while the people had the whole power in their own hands, and chose annually the Governor, the counselors, and the representatives. The people of old England had never enjoyed anything like the liberties and privileges which the settlers of New England now possessed. And they did not adopt these modes of government after long study, but in simplicity, as if there were no other way for people to be ruled.

"But, Laurence," continued Grandfather, "when you want instruction on these points you must seek it in Mr. Bancroft's History. I am merely telling the history of a chair. To proceed: the period during which the Governors sat in our chair was not very full of striking incidents. The province was now established on a secure foundation; but it did not increase so rapidly as at first, because the Puritans were no longer driven from England by persecution. However, there was still a quiet and natural growth. The legislature incorporated towns, and made new purchases of lands from the Indians. A very memorable event took place in 1643. The colonies of Massachusetts, Plymouth, Connecticut, and New Haven formed a union for the purpose of assisting each other in difficulties, for mutual defense against their enemies. They called themselves the United Colonies of New England."

"Were they under a government like that of the United States?" inquired Laurence.

"No," replied Grandfather; "the different

colonies did not compose one nation together; it was merely a confederacy among the governments. It somewhat resembled the league of the Amphictyons, which you remember in Grecian history. But to return to our chair. In 1644 it was highly honored; for Governor Endicott sat in it when he gave audience to an ambassador from the French governor of Acadia, or Nova Scotia. A treaty of peace between Massachusetts and the French colony was then signed."

"Did England allow Massachusetts to make war and peace with foreign countries?" asked Laurence.

"Massachusetts and the whole of New England was then almost independent of the mother country," said Grandfather. "There was now a civil war in England; and the king, as you may well suppose, had his hands full at home, and could pay but little attention to these remote colonies. When the Parliament got the power into their hands, they likewise had enough to do in keeping down the Cavaliers. Thus New England, like a young and hardy lad whose father and mother neglect it, was left to take care of itself. In 1649 King Charles was beheaded. Oliver Cromwell then became Protector of England; and as he was a Puritan himself, and had risen by the valor of the English Puritans, he showed himself a loving and indulgent father to the Puritan colonies in America."

Grandfather might have continued to talk in this dull manner nobody knows how long; but suspecting that Charley would find the subject rather dry, he looked sidewise at that vivacious little fellow, and saw him give an involuntary yawn. Whereupon Grandfather proceeded with the history of the chair, and related a very entertaining incident, which will be found in the next chapter.

CHAPTER VI

"ACCORDING to the most authentic records, my dear children," said Grandfather, "the chair, about this time, had the misfortune to break its leg. It was probably on account of this accident that it ceased to be the seat of the Governors of Massachusetts; for, assuredly, it would have been ominous of evil to the commonwealth if the Chair of State had tottered upon three legs. Being therefore sold at auction,—alas! what a vicissitude for a chair that had figured in such high company,—our venerable friend was knocked down to a certain Captain John Hull. This old gentleman, on carefully examining the maimed chair, discovered that its broken leg might be clamped with iron and made as serviceable as ever."

"Here is the very leg that was broken!" exclaimed Charley, throwing himself down on the floor to look at it. "And here are the iron clamps. How well it was mended!"

When they had all sufficiently examined the broken leg, Grandfather told them a story about Captain John Hull and

THE PINE-TREE SHILLINGS

The Captain John Hull aforesaid was the mint-master of Massachusetts, and coined all the money that was made there. This was a new line of business; for, in the earlier days of the colony, the current coinage consisted of gold and silver money of England, Portugal, and Spain. These coins being scarce, the people were often forced to barter their commodities instead of selling them.

For instance, if a man wanted to buy a coat, he perhaps exchanged a bear-skin for it. If he wished for a barrel of molasses, he might purchase it with a pile of pine boards. Musket-bullets were used instead of farthings. The Indians had a sort of money, called wampum, which was made of clam-shells; and this strange sort of specie was likewise taken in payment of debts by the English settlers. Bank-bills had never been heard of. There was not money enough of any kind, in many parts of the country, to pay the salaries of the ministers; so that they sometimes had to take quintals of fish, bushels of corn, or cords of wood, instead of silver or gold.

As the people grew more numerous, and their trade one with another increased, the want of current money was still more sensibly felt. To supply the demand, the general court passed a law for establishing a coinage of shillings, sixpences, and threepences. Captain John Hull was appointed to manufacture this money, and was to have about one shilling out of every twenty to pay him for the trouble of making them.

Hereupon all the old silver in the colony was handed over to Captain John Hull. The battered silver cans and tankards, I suppose, and silver buckles, and broken spoons, and silver buttons of worn-out coats, and silver hilts of swords that had figured at court,—all such curious old articles were doubtless thrown into the melting-pot together. But by far the greater part of the silver consisted of bullion from the mines of South America, which the English buccaneers—who were little better than pirates— had taken from the Spaniards and brought to Massachusetts.

All this old and new silver being melted down and coined, the result was an immense amount of splendid shillings, sixpences, and threepences. Each had the date, 1652, on the one side, and the figure of a pine-tree on the other.

Hence they were called pine-tree shillings. And for every twenty shillings that he coined, you will remember, Captain John Hull was entitled to put one shilling into his own pocket.

The magistrates soon began to suspect that the mint-master would have the best of the bargain. They offered him a large sum of money if he would but give up that twentieth shilling which he was continually dropping into his own pocket. But Captain Hull declared himself perfectly satisfied with the shilling. And well he might be; for so diligently did he labor that in a few years his pockets, his money-bags, and his strong box were overflowing with pine-tree shillings. This was probably the case when he came into possession of Grandfather's chair; and, as he had worked so hard at the mint, it was certainly proper that he should have a comfortable chair to rest himself in.

When the mint-master had grown very rich, a young man, Samuel Sewell by name, came a-courting to his only daughter. His daughter —whose name I do not know, but we will call her Betsey—was a fine, hearty damsel, by no means so slender as some young ladies of our own days. On the contrary, having always fed heartily on pumpkin pies, doughnuts, Indian puddings, and other Puritan dainties, she was as round and plump as a pudding herself. With this round, rosy Miss Betsey did Samuel

Sewell fall in love. As he was a young man of good character, industrious in his business, and a member of the church, the mint-master very readily gave his consent.

"Yes, you may take her," said he in his rough way, "and you'll find her a heavy burden enough!"

On the wedding day, we may suppose that honest John Hull dressed himself in a plum-colored coat, all the buttons of which were made of pine-tree shillings. The buttons of his waistcoat were sixpences; and the knees of his small-clothes were buttoned with silver threepences. Thus attired, he sat with great dignity in Grandfather's chair; and, being a portly old gentleman, he completely filled it from elbow to elbow. On the opposite side of the room, between her bridesmaids, sat Miss Betsey. She was blushing with all her might, and looked like a full-blown peony, or a great red apple.

There, too, was the bridegroom, dressed in a fine purple coat and gold lace waistcoat, with as much other finery as the Puritan laws and customs would allow him to put on. His hair was cropped close to his head, because Governor Endicott had forbidden any man to wear it below the ears. But he was a very personable young man, and so thought the bridesmaids, and Miss Betsey herself.

The mint-master also was pleased with his new

son-in-law, especially as he had courted Miss Betsey out of pure love, and had said nothing at all about her portion. So, when the marriage ceremony was over, Captain Hull whispered a word to two of his men-servants, who immediately went out, and soon returned, lugging a large pair of scales. They were such a pair as wholesale merchants use for weighing bulky commodities; and quite a bulky commodity was now to be weighed in them.

"Daughter Betsey," said the mint-master, "get into one side of these scales."

Miss Betsey—or Mrs. Sewell, as we must now call her—did as she was bid, like a dutiful child, without any question of the why and wherefore. But what her father could mean, unless to make her husband pay for her by the pound (in which case she would have been a dear bargain), she had not the least idea.

"And now," said honest John Hull to the servants, "bring that box hither."

The box to which the mint-master pointed was a huge, square, iron-bound, oaken chest; it was big enough, my children, for all four of you to play at hide-and-seek in. The servants tugged with might and main, but could not lift this enormous receptacle, and were finally obliged to drag it across the floor. Captain Hull then took a key from his girdle, unlocked the chest, and lifted its ponderous lid. Behold! it was full to the brim of bright pine-tree shillings, fresh from the mint; and Samuel Sewell began to think that his father-in-law had got possession of all the money in the Massachusetts treasury. But it was only the mint-master's honest share of the coinage.

Then the servants, at Captain Hull's command, heaped double handfuls of shillings into one side of the scales, while Betsey remained in the other. Jingle, jingle, went the shillings, as handful after handful was thrown in, till, plump and ponderous as she was, they fairly weighed the young lady from the floor.

"There, son Sewell!" cried the honest mint-master, resuming his seat in Grandfather's chair, "take these shillings for my daughter's portion. Use her kindly, and thank Heaven for her. It is not every wife that's worth her weight in silver!"

The children laughed heartily at this legend, and would hardly be convinced but that Grandfather had made it out of his own head. He assured them faithfully, however, that he had found it in the pages of a grave historian, and had merely tried to tell it in a somewhat funnier style. As for Samuel Sewell, he afterward became Chief Justice of Massachusetts.

"Well, Grandfather," remarked Clara, "if

wedding portions nowadays were paid as Miss Betsey's was, young ladies would not pride themselves upon an airy figure, as many of them do."

CHAPTER VII

WHEN his little audience next assembled round the chair, Grandfather gave them a doleful history of the Quaker persecution, which began in 1656, and raged for about three years in Massachusetts.

He told them how, in the first place, twelve of the converts of George Fox, the first Quaker in the world, had come over from England. They seemed to be impelled by an earnest love for the souls of men, and a pure desire to make known what they considered a revelation from Heaven. But the rulers looked upon them as plotting the downfall of all government and religion. They were banished from the colony. In a little while, however, not only the first twelve had returned, but a multitude of other Quakers had come to rebuke the rulers and to preach against the priests and steeple-houses.

Grandfather described the hatred and scorn with which these enthusiasts were received. They were thrown into dungeons; they were beaten with many stripes, women as well as men; they were driven forth into the wilderness, and left to the tender mercies of wild beasts and Indians. The children were amazed to hear that the more the Quakers were scourged, and imprisoned, and banished, the more did the sect increase, both by the influx of strangers and by converts from among the Puritans. But Grandfather told them that God had put something into the soul of man which always turned the cruelties of the persecutor to nought.

He went on to relate that, in 1659, two Quakers, named William Robinson and Marmaduke Stephenson, were hanged at Boston. A woman had been sentenced to die with them, but was reprieved on condition of her leaving the colony. Her name was Mary Dyer. In the year 1660 she returned to Boston, although she knew death awaited her there; and, if Grandfather had been correctly informed, an incident had then taken place which connects her with our story. This Mary Dyer had entered the mint-master's dwelling, clothed in sackcloth and ashes, and seated herself in our great chair with a sort of dignity and state. Then she proceeded to deliver what she called a message from Heaven, but in the midst of it they dragged her to prison.

"And was she executed?" asked Laurence.

"She was," said Grandfather.

"Grandfather," cried Charley, clinching his

fist, "I would have fought for that poor Quaker woman!"

"Ah! but if a sword had been drawn for her," said Laurence, "it would have taken away all the beauty of her death."

It seemed as if hardly any of the preceding stories had thrown such an interest around Grandfather's chair as did the fact that the poor, persecuted, wandering Quaker woman had rested in it for a moment. The children were so much excited that Grandfather found it necessary to bring his account of the persecution to a close.

"In 1660, the same year in which Mary Dyer was executed," said he, "Charles the Second was restored to the throne of his fathers. This king had many vices; but he would not permit blood to be shed, under pretense of religion, in any part of his dominions. The Quakers in Enggland told him what had been done to their brethren in Massachusetts; and he sent orders to Governor Endicott to forbear all such proceedings in future. And so ended the Quaker persecution,—one of the most mournful passages in the history of our forefathers."

Grandfather then told his auditors that, shortly after the above incident, the great chair had been given by the mint-master to the Rev. Mr. John Eliot. He was the first minister of Roxbury. But besides attending to the pastoral duties there, he learned the language of the red men, and often went into the woods to preach to them. So earnestly did he labor for their conversion that he has always been called the Apostle to the Indians. The mention of this holy man suggested to Grandfather the propriety of giving a brief sketch of the history of the Indians, so far as they were connected with the English colonists.

A short period before the arrival of the first Pilgrims at Plymouth there had been a very grievous plague among the red men; and the sages and ministers of that day were inclined to the opinion that Providence had sent this mortality in order to make room for the settlement of the English. But I know not why we should suppose that an Indian's life is less precious, in the eye of Heaven, than that of a white man. Be that as it may, death had certainly been very busy with the savage tribes.

In many places the English found the wigwams deserted and the cornfields going to waste, with none to harvest the grain. There were heaps of earth also, which, being dug open, proved to be Indian graves, containing bows and flint-headed spears and arrows; for the Indians buried the dead warrior's weapons along with him. In some spots there were skulls and other human bones lying unburied. In 1633, and the year afterward, the smallpox broke out among the Massachusetts Indians, multitudes of whom died by this terrible disease of the Old World. These misfortunes made them far less powerful than they had formerly been.

For nearly half a century after the arrival of the English the red men showed themselves generally inclined to peace and amity. They often made submission when they might have made successful war. The Plymouth settlers, led by the famous Captain Miles Standish, slew some of them, in 1623, without any very evident necessity for so doing. In 1636, and the following year, there was the most dreadful war that had yet occurred between the Indians and the English. The Connecticut settlers, assisted by a celebrated Indian chief named Uncas, bore the brunt of this war, with but little aid from Massachusetts. Many hundreds of the hostile Indians were slain or burned in their wigwams. Sassacus, their sachem, fled to another tribe, after his own people were defeated; but he was murdered by them, and his head was sent to his English enemies.

From that period down to the time of King Philip's war, which will be mentioned hereafter, there was not much trouble with the Indians. But the colonists were always on their guard, and kept their weapons ready for the conflict.

"I have sometimes doubted," said Grandfather, when he had told these things to the children, "I have sometimes doubted whether there was more than a single man among our forefathers, who realized that an Indian possesses a mind, and a heart, and an immortal soul. That single man was John Eliot. All the rest of the early settlers seemed to think that the Indians were an inferior race of beings, whom the Creator had merely allowed to keep possession of this beautiful country till the white men should be in want of it."

"Did the pious men of those days never try to make Christians of them?" asked Laurence.

"Sometimes, it is true," answered Grandfather, "the magistrates and ministers would talk about civilizing and converting the red people. But, at the bottom of their hearts, they would have had almost as much expectation of civilizing the wild bear of the woods and making him fit for paradise. They felt no faith in the success of any such attempts, because they had no love for the poor Indians. Now, Eliot was full of love for them; and therefore so full of faith and hope that he spent the labor of a lifetime in their behalf."

"I would have conquered them first, and then converted them," said Charley.

"Ah, Charley! there spoke the very spirit of our forefathers!" replied Grandfather. "But Mr. Eliot had a better spirit. He looked upon them as his brethren. He persuaded as many of them as he could to leave off their idle and wandering habits, and to build houses and cultivate the earth, as the English did. He established schools among them and taught many of the Indians how to read. He taught them, likewise, how to pray. Hence they were called 'praying Indians.' Finally, having spent the best years of his life for their good, Mr. Eliot resolved to spend the remainder in doing them a yet greater benefit."

"I know what that was!" cried Laurence.

"He sat down in his study," continued Grandfather, "and began a translation of the Bible into the Indian tongue. It was while he was engaged in this pious work that the mint-master gave him our great chair. His toil needed it and deserved it."

"Oh, Grandfather, tell us all about that Indian Bible!" exclaimed Laurence. "I have seen it in the library of the Athenæum; and the tears came into my eyes to think that there were no Indians left to read it."

CHAPTER VIII

As Grandfather was a great admirer of the Apostle Eliot, he was glad to comply with the earnest request which Laurence had made at the close of the last chapter. So he proceeded to describe how good Mr. Eliot labored while he was at work upon

THE INDIAN BIBLE

My dear children, what a task would you think it, even with a long lifetime before you, were you bidden to copy every chapter, and verse, and word in yonder family Bible! Would not this be a heavy toil? But if the task were, not to write off the English Bible, but to learn a language utterly unlike all other tongues—a language which hitherto had never been learned, except by the Indians themselves, from their mothers' lips—a language never written, and the strange words of which seemed inexpressible by letters;—if the task were, first to learn this new variety of speech, and then to translate the Bible into it, and to do it so carefully that not one idea throughout the holy book should be changed—what would induce you to undertake this toil? Yet this was what the Apostle Eliot did.

It was a mighty work for a man, now growing old, to take upon himself. And what earthly reward could he expect from it? None; no reward on earth. But he believed that the red men were the descendants of those lost tribes of Israel of whom history has been able to tell us nothing for thousands of years. He hoped that God had sent the English across the ocean, Gentiles as they were, to enlighten this benighted portion of his once chosen race. And when he should be summoned hence, he trusted to meet blessed spirits in another world, whose bliss would have been earned by his patient toil in translating the Word of God. This hope and trust were far dearer to him than anything that earth could offer.

Sometimes, while thus at work, he was visited by learned men, who desired to know what literary undertaking Mr. Eliot had in hand. They, like himself, had been bred in the studious cloisters of a university, and were supposed to possess all the erudition which mankind has hoarded up from age to age. Greek and Latin were as familiar to them as the babble of their childhood. Hebrew was like their mother tongue. They had grown gray in study; their eyes were bleared with pouring over print and manuscript by the light of the midnight lamp.

And yet, how much had they left unlearned! Mr. Eliot would put into their hands some of the pages which he had been writing; and behold! the gray-headed men stammered over the long, strange words, like a little child in his first attempts to read. Then would the apostle call to him an Indian boy, one of his scholars, and show him the manuscript which had so puzzled the learned Englishmen.

"Read this, my child," said he; "these are

some brethren of mine, who would fain hear the sound of thy native tongue."

Then would the Indian boy cast his eyes over the mysterious page, and read it so skillfully that it sounded like wild music. It seemed as if the forest leaves were singing in the ears of his auditors, and as if the roar of distant streams were poured through the young Indian's voice. Such were the sounds amid which the language of the red men had been formed; and they were still heard to echo in it.

The lesson being over, Mr. Eliot would give the Indian boy an apple or a cake, and bid him leap forth into the open air which his free nature loved. The apostle was kind to children, and even shared in their sports sometimes. And when his visitors had bidden him farewell, the good man turned patiently to his toil again.

No other Englishman had ever understood the Indian character so well, nor possessed so great an influence over the New England tribes, as the apostle did. His advice and assistance must often have been valuable to his countrymen, in their transactions with the Indians. Occasionally, perhaps, the Governor and some of the counselors came to visit Mr. Eliot. Perchance they were seeking some method to circumvent the forest people. They inquired, it may be, how they could obtain possession of such and such a tract of their rich land. Or they talked

of making the Indians their servants, as if God
had destined them for perpetual bondage to the
more powerful white man.

Perhaps, too, some warlike captain, dressed in
his buff-coat, with a corselet beneath it, accompanied the Governor and counselors. Laying
his hand upon his sword-hilt, he would declare
that the only method of dealing with the red men
was to meet them with the sword drawn and
the musket presented.

But the apostle resisted both the craft of the
politician and the fierceness of the warrior.

"Treat these sons of the forest as men and
brethren," he would say, "and let us endeavor
to make them Christians. Their forefathers were
of that chosen race whom God delivered from
Egyptian bondage. Perchance he has destined
us to deliver the children from the more cruel
bondage of ignorance and idolatry. Chiefly for
this end, it may be, we were directed across the
ocean."

When these other visitors were gone, Mr. Eliot
bent himself again over the half-written page.
He dared hardly relax a moment from his toil.
He felt that, in the book which he was translating,
there was a deep human as well as heavenly
wisdom, which would of itself suffice to civilize
and refine the savage tribes. Let the Bible be
diffused among them, and all earthly good would
follow. But how slight a consideration was this,

when he reflected that the eternal welfare of a whole race of men depended upon his accomplishment of the task which he had set himself! What if his hand should be palsied? What if his mind should lose its vigor? What if death should come upon him ere the work were done? Then must the red man wander in the dark wilderness of heathenism forever.

Impelled by such thoughts as these, he sat writing in the great chair when the pleasant summer breeze came in through his open casement; and also when the fire of forest logs sent up its blaze and smoke, through the broad stone chimney, into the wintry air. Before the earliest bird sang in the morning the apostle's lamp was kindled; and, at midnight, his weary head was not yet upon its pillow. And at length, leaning back in the great chair, he could say to himself, with a holy triumph: "The work is finished!"

It was finished. Here was a Bible for the Indians. Those long-lost descendants of the ten tribes of Israel would now learn the history of their forefathers. That grace which the ancient Israelites had forfeited was offered anew to their children.

There is no impiety in believing that, when his long life was over, the apostle of the Indians was welcomed to the celestial abodes of the prophets of ancient days, and by those earliest apostles and evangelists who had drawn their inspiration from the immediate presence of the Saviour. They first had preached truth and salvation to the world. And Eliot, separated from them by many centuries, yet full of the same spirit, had borne the like message to the New World of the West. Since the first days of Christianity, there has been no man more worthy to be numbered in the brotherhood of the apostles than Eliot.

"My heart is not satisfied to think," observed Laurence, "that Mr. Eliot's labors have done no good except to a few Indians of his own time. Doubtless he would not have regretted his toil, if it were the means of saving but a single soul. But it is a grievous thing to me that he should have toiled so hard to translate the Bible, and now the language and the people are gone! The Indian Bible itself is almost the only relic of both."

"Laurence," said his Grandfather, "if ever you should doubt that man is capable of disinterested zeal for his brother's good, then remember how the apostle Eliot toiled. And if you should feel your own self-interest pressing upon your heart too closely, then think of Eliot's Indian Bible. It is good for the world that such a man has lived and left this emblem of his life."

The tears gushed into the eyes of Laurence, and he acknowledged that Eliot had not toiled in vain. Little Alice put up her arms to Grandfather, and drew down his white head beside her own golden locks.

"Grandfather," whispered she, "I want to kiss good Mr. Eliot!"

And, doubtless, good Mr. Eliot would gladly receive the kiss of so sweet a child as little Alice, and would think it a portion of his reward in heaven.

Grandfather now observed that Dr. Francis had written a very beautiful Life of Eliot which he advised Laurence to peruse. He then spoke of King Philip's War, which began in 1675, and terminated with the death of King Philip, in the following year. Philip was a proud, fierce Indian, whom Mr. Eliot had vainly endeavored to convert to the Christian faith.

"It must have been a great anguish to the apostle," continued Grandfather, "to hear of mutual slaughter and outrage between his own countrymen and those for whom he felt the affection of a father. A few of the praying Indians joined the followers of King Philip. A greater number fought on the side of the English. In the course of the war the little community of red people whom Mr. Eliot had begun to civilize was scattered, and probably never was restored to a flourishing condition. But his zeal did not grow cold; and only about five years before his death he took great pains in preparing a new edition of the Indian Bible."

"I do wish, Grandfather," cried Charley,

"you would tell us all about the battles in King Philip's War."

"Oh, no!" exclaimed Clara. "Who wants to hear about tomahawks and scalping-knives?"

"No, Charley," replied Grandfather, "I have no time to spare in talking about battles. You must be content with knowing that it was the bloodiest war that the Indians had ever waged against the white men; and that, at its close, the English set King Philip's head upon a pole."

"Who was the captain of the English?" asked Charley.

"Their most noted captain was Benjamin Church,—a very famous warrior," said Grandfather. "But I assure you, Charley, that neither Captain Church, nor any of the officers and soldiers who fought in King Philip's War, did anything a thousandth part so glorious as Mr. Eliot did when he translated the Bible for the Indians."

"Let Laurence be the apostle," said Charley to himself, "and I will be the captain."

CHAPTER IX

THE children were now accustomed to assemble round Grandfather's chair at all their unoccupied moments; and often it was a striking picture to behold the whited-headed old sire,

with this flowery wreath of young people around
him. When he talked to them, it was the past
speaking to the present, or rather to the future,—
for the children were of a generation which had
not become actual. Their part in life, thus far,
was only to be happy and to draw knowledge
from a thousand sources. As yet, it was not
their time to do.

Sometimes, as Grandfather gazed at their
fair, unworldly countenances a mist of tears
bedimmed his spectacles. He almost regretted
that it was necessary for them to know anything
of the past or to provide aught for the future.
He could have wished that they might be always
the happy, youthful creatures who had hitherto
sported around his chair, without inquiring
whether it had a history. It grieved him to
think that his little Alice, who was a flower-bud
fresh from paradise, must open her leaves to the
rough breezes of the world, or ever open them
in any clime. So sweet a child she was, that it
seemed fit her infancy should be immortal!

But such repinings were merely flitting
shadows across the old man's heart. He had
faith enough to believe, and wisdom enough to
know, that the bloom of the flower would be
even holier and happier˙ than its bud. Even
within himself—though Grandfather was now
at that period of life when the veil of mortality
is apt to hang heavily over the soul—still, in

his inmost being he was conscious of something
that he would not have exchanged for the best
happiness of childhood. It was a bliss to which
every sort of earthly experience—all that he had
enjoyed, or suffered, or seen, or heard, or acted,
with the broodings of his soul upon the whole—
had contributed somewhat. In the same manner
must a bliss, of which now they could have no
conception, grow up within these children, and
form a part of their sustenance for immortality.

So Grandfather, with renewed cheerfulness,
continued his history of the chair, trusting that
a profounder wisdom than his own would extract, from these flowers and weeds of Time, a
fragrance that might last beyond all time.

At this period of the story Grandfather threw
a glance backward as far as the year 1660. He
spoke of the ill-concealed reluctance with which
the Puritans in America had acknowledged the
sway of Charles the Second on his restoration
to his father's throne. When death had stricken
Oliver Cromwell, that mighty Protector had no
sincerer mourners than in New England. The
new king had been more than a year upon
the throne before his accession was proclaimed
in Boston; although the neglect to perform the
ceremony might have subjected the rulers to the
charge of treason.

During the reign of Charles the Second,
however, the American colonies had but little

reason to complain of harsh or tyrannical treatment. But when Charles died, in 1685, and was succeeded by his brother James, the patriarchs of New England began to tremble. King James was a bigoted Roman Catholic, and was known to be of an arbitrary temper. It was feared by all Protestants, and chiefly by the Puritans, that he would assume despotic power and attempt to establish Popery throughout his dominions. Our forefathers felt that they had no security either for their religion or their liberties.

The result proved that they had reason for their apprehensions. King James caused the charters of all the American colonies to be taken away. The old charter of Massachusetts, which the people regarded as a holy thing and as the foundation of all their liberties, was declared void. The colonists were now no longer freemen; they were entirely dependent on the king's pleasure. At first, in 1685, King James appointed Joseph Dudley, a native of Massachusetts, to be president of New England. But soon afterward Sir Edmund Andros, an officer of the English army, arrived, with a commission to be Governor-general of New England and New York.

The king had given such powers to Sir Edmund Andros that there was now no liberty, nor scarcely any law, in the colonies over which he ruled. The inhabitants were not allowed to choose representatives, and consequently had no voice whatever in the government, nor control over the measures that were adopted. The counselors with whom the Governor consulted on matters of state were appointed by himself. This sort of government was no better than an absolute despotism.

"The people suffered much wrong while Sir Edmund Andros ruled over them," continued Grandfather; "and they were apprehensive of much more. He had brought some soldiers with him from England, who took possession of the old fortress on Castle Island and of the fortification on Fort Hill. Sometimes it was rumored that a general massacre of the inhabitants was to be perpetrated by these soldiers. There were reports, too, that all the ministers were to be slain or imprisoned."

"For what?" inquired Charley.

"Because they were the leaders of the people, Charley," said Grandfather. "A minister was a more formidable man than a general in those days. Well; while these things were going on in America, King James had so misgoverned the people of England that they sent over to Holland for the Prince of Orange. He had married the king's daughter, and was therefore considered to have a claim to the crown. On his arrival in England, the Prince of Orange was proclaimed king, by the name of William the Third. Poor old King James made his escape to France."

Grandfather told how, at the first intelligence of the landing of the Prince of Orange in England, the people of Massachusetts rose in their strength and overthrew the government of Sir Edmund Andros. He, with Joseph Dudley, Edmund Randolph, and his other principal adherents, was thrown into prison. Old Simon Bradstreet, who had been Governor when King James took away the charter, was called by the people to govern them again.

"Governor Bradstreet was a venerable old man, nearly ninety years of age," said Grandfather. "He came over with the first settlers, and had been the intimate companion of all those excellent and famous men who laid the foundation of our country. They were all gone before him to the grave; and Bradstreet was the last of the Puritans."

Grandfather paused a moment and smiled, as if he had something very interesting to tell his auditors. He then proceeded:

"And now, Laurence,—now Clara,—now, Charley,—now, my dear little Alice,—what chair do you think had been placed in the council chamber for old Governor Bradstreet to take his seat in? Would you believe that it was this very chair in which Grandfather now sits, and of which he is telling you the history?"

"I am glad to hear it, with all my heart!" cried Charley, after a shout of delight. "I thought Grandfather had quite forgotten the chair."

"It was a solemn and affecting sight," said Grandfather, "when this venerable patriarch, with his white beard flowing down upon his breast, took his seat in his Chair of State. Within his remembrance, and even since his mature age, the site where now stood the populous town had been a wild and forest-covered peninsula. The province, now so fertile and spotted with thriving villages, had been a desert wilderness. He was surrounded by a shouting multitude, most of whom had been born in the country which he had helped to found. They were of one generation, and he of another. As the old man looked upon them, and beheld new faces everywhere, he must have felt that it was now time for him to go whither his brethren had gone before him."

"Were the former Governors all dead and gone?" asked Laurence.

"All of them," replied Grandfather. "Winthrop had been dead forty years. Endicott died, a very old man, in 1665. Sir Henry Vane was beheaded, in London, at the beginning of the reign of Charles the Second. And Haynes, Dudley, Bellingham, and Leverett, who had all been Governors of Massachusetts, were now likewise in their graves. Old Simon Bradstreet was the sole representative of that departed brotherhood. There was no other public man remaining to connect the ancient system of government and manners with the new system which was about to take its place. The era of the Puritans was now completed."

"I am sorry for it," observed Laurence; "for, though they were so stern, yet it seems to me that there was something warm and real about them. I think, Grandfather, that each of these old Governors should have his statue set up in our State House, sculptured out of the hardest of New England granite."

"It would not be amiss, Laurence," said Grandfather; "but perhaps clay, or some other perishable material, might suffice for some of their successors. But let us go back to our chair. It was occupied by Governor Bradstreet from April, 1689, until May, 1692. Sir William Phips then arrived in Boston, with a new charter from King William and a commission to be Governor."

CHAPTER X

"AND what became of the chair?" inquired Clara.

"The outward aspect of our chair," replied Grandfather, "was now somewhat the worse for its long and arduous services. It was considered hardly magnificent enough to be allowed to keep its place in the council chamber of Massachusetts. In fact, it was banished as an article of useless lumber. But Sir William Phips happened to see it, and, being much pleased with its construction, resolved to take the good old chair into his private mansion. Accordingly, with his own gubernatorial hands, he repaired one of its arms, which had been slightly damaged."

"Why, Grandfather, here is the very arm!" interrupted Charley, in great wonderment. "And did Sir William Phips put in these screws with his own hands? I am sure he did it beautifully! But how came a Governor to know how to mend a chair?"

"I will tell you a story about the early life of Sir William Phips," said Grandfather. "You will then perceive that he well knew how to use his hands."

So Grandfather related the wonderful and true tale of

THE SUNKEN TREASURE

Picture to yourselves, my dear children, a handsome, old-fashioned room, with a large, open cupboard at one end, in which is displayed a magnificent gold cup, with some other splendid articles of gold and silver plate. In another part of the room, opposite to a tall looking-glass, stands our beloved chair, newly polished, and adorned with a gorgeous cushion of crimson velvet, tufted with gold.

In the chair sits a man of strong and sturdy frame, whose face has been roughened by northern tempests and blackened by the burning sun of the West Indies. He wears an immense periwig, flowing down over his shoulders. His coat has a wide embroidery of golden foliage; and his waistcoat, likewise, is all flowered over and bedizened with gold. His red, rough hands, which have done many a good day's work with the hammer and adze, are half covered by the delicate lace ruffles at his wrists. On a table lies his silver-hilted sword; and in the corner of the room stands his gold-headed cane, made of a beautifully polished West India wood.

Somewhat such an aspect as this did Sir William Phips present when he sat in Grandfather's chair after the king had appointed him Governor of Massachusetts. Truly, there was need that the old chair should be varnished and decorated with a crimson cushion in order to make it suitable for such a magnificent looking personage.

But Sir William Phips had not always worn a gold-embroidered coat, nor always sat so much at his ease as he did in Grandfather's chair. He was a poor man's son, and was born in the province of Maine, where he used to tend sheep upon the hills in his boyhood and youth. Until he had grown to be a man, he did not even know how to read and write. Tired of tending sheep, he next apprenticed himself to a ship-carpenter, and spent about four years in hewing the crooked limbs of oak trees into knees for vessels.

In 1673, when he was twenty-two years old, he came to Boston, and soon afterward was married to a widow lady, who had property enough to set him up in business. It was not long, however, before he lost all the money that he had acquired by his marriage, and became a poor man again. Still, he was not discouraged. He often told his wife that, some time or other, he should be very rich, and would build a "fair brick house" in the Green Lane of Boston.

Do not suppose, children, that he had been to a fortune-teller to inquire his destiny. It was his own energy and spirit of enterprise, and his resolution to lead an industrious life, that made him look forward with so much confidence to better days.

Several years passed away, and William Phips had not yet gained the riches which he promised to himself. During this time he had begun to follow the sea for a living. In the year 1684 he happened to hear of a Spanish ship which had been cast away near the Bahama Islands, and which was supposed to contain a great deal of gold and silver. Phips went to the place in a small vessel, hoping that he should be able to recover some of the treasure from the wreck.

He did not succeed, however, in fishing up gold and silver enough to pay the expenses of his voyage.

But, before he returned, he was told of another Spanish ship, or galleon, which had been cast away near Porto de la Plata. She had now lain as much as fifty years beneath the waves. This old ship had been laden with immense wealth; and, hitherto, nobody had thought of the possibility of recovering any part of it from the deep sea which was rolling and tossing it about. But though it was now an old story, and the most aged people had almost forgotten that such a vessel had been wrecked, William Phips resolved that the sunken treasure should again be brought to light.

He went to London and obtained admittance to King James, who had not yet been driven from his throne. He told the king of the vast wealth that was lying at the bottom of the sea. King James listened with attention, and thought this a fine opportunity to fill his treasury with Spanish gold. He appointed William Phips to be captain of a vessel called the *Rose Algier*, carrying eighteen guns and ninety-five men. So now he was Captain Phips of the English Navy.

Captain Phips sailed from England in the *Rose Algier*, and cruised for nearly two years in the West Indies, endeavoring to find the wreck of the Spanish ship. But the sea is so wide and deep that it is no easy matter to discover the exact spot where a sunken vessel lies. The prospect of success seemed very small; and most people would have thought that Captain Phips was as far from having money enough to build a "fair brick house" as he was while he tended sheep.

The seamen of the *Rose Algier* became discouraged, and gave up all hope of making their fortunes by discovering the Spanish wreck. They wanted to compel Captain Phips to turn pirate. There was a much better prospect, they thought, of growing rich by plundering vessels which still sailed in the sea than by seeking for a ship that had lain beneath the waves full half a century. They broke out in open mutiny, but were finally mastered by Phips, and compelled to obey his orders. It would have been dangerous, however, to continue much longer at sea with such a crew of mutinous sailors; and, besides, the *Rose Algier* was leaky and unseaworthy. So Captain Phips judged it best to return to England.

Before leaving the West Indies, he met with a Spaniard, an old man, who remembered the wreck of the Spanish ship, and gave him directions how to find the very spot. It was on a reef of rocks, a few leagues from Porto de la Plata.

On his arrival in England, therefore, Captain Phips solicited the king to let him have another vessel and send him back again to the West Indies. But King James, who had probably expected that the *Rose Algier* would return laden with gold, refused to have anything more to do with the affair. Phips might never have been able to renew the search if the Duke of Albemarle and some other noblemen had not lent their assistance. They fitted out a ship, and gave the command to Captain Phips. He sailed from England, and arrived safely at Porto de la Plata, where he took an adze and assisted his men to build a large boat.

The boat was intended for the purpose of going closer to the reef of rocks than a large vessel could safely venture. When it was finished, the captain sent several men in it to examine the spot where the Spanish ship was said to have been wrecked. They were accompanied by some Indians, who were skillful divers, and could go down a great way into the depths of the sea.

The boat's crew proceeded to the reef of rocks, and rowed round and round it a great many times. They gazed down into the water, which was so transparent that it seemed as if they could have seen the gold and silver at the bottom, had there been any of those precious metals there. Nothing, however, could they see; nothing more valuable than a curious sea shrub, which was growing beneath the water, in a crevice of the reef of rocks. It flaunted to and fro with the swell and reflux of the waves, and looked as bright and beautiful as if its leaves were gold.

"We won't go back empty-handed," cried an English sailor; and then he spoke to one of the Indian divers. "Dive down and bring me that pretty sea shrub there. That's the only treasure we shall find!"

Down plunged the diver, and soon rose dripping from the water, holding the sea shrub in his hand. But he had learnt some news at the bottom of the sea.

"There are some ship's guns," said he, the moment he had drawn breath, "some great cannon, among the rocks, near where the shrub was growing."

No sooner had he spoken than the English sailors knew that they had found the very spot where the Spanish galleon had been wrecked, so many years before. The other Indian divers immediately plunged over the boat's side and swam headlong down, groping among the rocks and sunken cannon. In a few moments one of them rose above the water with a heavy lump of silver in his arms. That single lump was worth more than a thousand dollars. The sailors took it into the boat, and then rowed back as speedily as they could, being in haste to inform Captain Phips of their good luck.

But, confidently as the captain had hoped to find the Spanish wreck, yet now that it was really found, the news seemed too good to be true. He could not believe it till the sailors showed him the lump of silver.

"Thanks be to God!" then cries Captain Phips. "We shall every man of us make our fortunes!"

Hereupon the captain and all the crew set to work, with iron rakes and great hooks and lines, fishing for gold and silver at the bottom of the sea. Up came the treasure in abundance. Now they beheld a table of solid silver, once the property of an old Spanish grandee. Now they found a sacramental vessel, which had been destined as a gift to some Catholic church. Now they drew up a golden cup, fit for the king of Spain to drink his wine out of. Perhaps the bony hand of its former owner had been grasping the precious cup, and was drawn up along with it. Now their rakes or fishing-lines were loaded with masses of silver bullion. There were also precious stones among the treasure, glittering and sparkling, so that it is a wonder how their radiance could have been concealed.

There is something sad and terrible in the idea of snatching all this wealth from the devouring ocean, which had possessed it for such a length of years. It seems as if men had no right to make themselves rich with it. It ought to have been left with the skeletons of the ancient Spaniards, who had been drowned when the ship was wrecked, and whose bones were now scattered among the gold and silver.

But Captain Phips and his crew were troubled with no such thoughts as these. After a day or two they lighted on another part of the wreck, where they found a great many bags of silver dollars. But nobody could have guessed that these were money-bags. By remaining so long in the salt-water, they had become covered over with a crust which had the appearance of stone, so that it was necessary to break them in pieces with hammers and axes. When this was done, a stream of silver dollars gushed out upon the deck of the vessel.

The whole value of the recovered treasure, plate, bullion, precious stones, and all, was estimated at more than two millions of dollars. It was dangerous even to look at such a vast amount of wealth. A sea captain, who had assisted Phips in the enterprise, utterly lost his reason at the sight of it. He died two years afterward, still raving about the treasures that lie at the bottom of the sea. It would have been better for this man if he had left the skeletons of the shipwrecked Spaniards in quiet possession of their wealth.

Captain Phips and his men continued to fish up plate, bullion, and dollars, as plentifully as ever, till their provisions grew short. Then, as they could not feed upon gold and silver any more than old King Midas could, they found it necessary to go in search of better sustenance. Phips resolved to return to England. He arrived there in 1687, and was received with great joy by the Duke of Albemarle and other English lords who had fitted out the vessel. Well they might rejoice; for they took by far the greater part of the treasure to themselves.

The captain's share, however, was enough to make him comfortable for the rest of his days. It also enabled him to fulfill his promise to his wife, by building a "fair brick house" in the Green Lane of Boston. The Duke of Albemarle sent Mrs. Phips a magnificent gold cup, worth at least five thousand dollars. Before Captain Phips left London, King James made him a knight; so that, instead of the obscure ship-carpenter who had formerly dwelt among them, the inhabitants of Boston welcomed him on his return as the rich and famous Sir William Phips.

CHAPTER XI

"SIR WILLIAM PHIPS," continued Grandfather, "was too active and adventurous a man to sit still in the quiet enjoyment of his good fortune. In the year 1690 he went on a military expedition against the French colonies in America, conquered the whole province of Acadia, and returned to Boston with a great deal of plunder."

"Why, Grandfather, he was the greatest man that ever sat in the chair!" cried Charley.

"Ask Laurence what he thinks," replied Grandfather, with a smile. "Well; in the same year, Sir William took command of an expedition against Quebec, but did not succeed in capturing the city. In 1692, being then in London, King William the Third appointed him Governor of Massachusetts. And now, my dear children, having followed Sir William Phips through all his adventures and hardships till we find him comfortably seated in Grandfather's chair, we will here bid him farewell. May he be as happy in ruling a people as he was while he tended sheep!"

Charley, whose fancy had been greatly taken by the adventurous disposition of Sir William Phips, was eager to know how he had acted and what happened to him while he held the office of Governor. But Grandfather had made up his mind to tell no more stories for the present.

"Possibly, one of these days, I may go on with the adventures of the chair," said he. "But its history becomes very obscure just at this point; and I must search into some old books and manuscripts before proceeding further. Besides, it is now a good time to pause in our narrative; because the new charter, which Sir William Phips brought over from England, formed a very important epoch in the history of the province."

"Really, Grandfather," observed Laurence, "this seems to be the most remarkable chair in the world. Its history cannot be told without intertwining it with the lives of distinguished men and the great events that have befallen the country."

"True, Laurence," replied Grandfather, smiling. "We must write a book with some such title as this,—MEMOIRS OF MY OWN TIMES, BY GRANDFATHER'S CHAIR."

"That would be beautiful!" exclaimed Laurence, clapping his hands.

"But, after all," continued Grandfather, "any other old chair, if it possessed memory and a hand to write its recollections, could record stranger stories than any that I have told you. From generation to generation, a chair sits familiarly in the midst of human interests, and is witness to the most secret and confidential intercourse that mortal man can hold with his fellow. The human heart may best be read in the fireside chair. And as to external events, Grief and Joy keep a continual vicissitude around it and within it. Now we see the glad face and glowing form of Joy, sitting merrily in the old chair, and throwing a warm fire-light radiance over all the household. Now, while we thought not of it, the dark-clad mourner, Grief, has stolen into the place of Joy, but not to retain it long. The imagination can hardly grasp so wide a subject as is embraced in the experience of a family chair."

"It makes my breath flutter, my heart thrill, to think of it," said Laurence. "Yes; a family chair must have a deeper history than a Chair of State."

"Oh, yes!" cried Clara, expressing a woman's feeling on the point in question; "the history of a country is not nearly so interesting as that of a single family would be."

"But the history of a country is more easily told," said Grandfather. "So, if we proceed with our narrative of the chair, I shall still confine myself to its connection with public events."

Good old Grandfather now rose and quitted the room, while the children remained gazing at the chair. Laurence, so vivid was his conception of past times, would hardly have deemed it strange if its former occupants, one after another, had resumed the seat which they had each left vacant such a dim length of years ago.

First, the gentle and lovely Lady Arbella would have been seen in the old chair, almost sinking out of its arms for very weakness; then Roger Williams, in his cloak and band, earnest, energetic, and benevolent; then the figure of Anne Hutchinson, with the like gesture as when she presided at the assemblages of women; then the dark, intellectual face of Vane, "young in years, but in sage counsel old." Next would have appeared the successive Governors, Winthrop, Dudley, Bellingham, and Endicott, who sat in the chair while it was a Chair of State. Then its ample seat would have been pressed by the comfortable, rotund corporation of the honest mint-master. Then the half-frenzied shape of Mary Dyer, the persecuted Quaker woman, clad in sackcloth and ashes, would have rested in it for a moment. Then the holy apostolic form of Eliot would have sanctified it. Then would have arisen, like the shade of departed Puritanism, the venerable dignity of the white-bearded Governor Bradstreet. Lastly, on the gorgeous crimson cushion of Grandfather's chair, would have shone the purple and golden magnificence of Sir William Phips.

But all these, with the other historic personages in the midst of whom the chair had so often stood, had passed, both in substance and shadow, from the scene of ages! Yet here stood the chair, with the old Lincoln coat of arms, and the oaken flowers and foliage, and the fierce lion's head at the summit, the whole, apparently, in as perfect preservation as when it had first been placed in the Earl of Lincoln's hall. And what vast changes of society and of nations had been wrought by sudden convulsions or by slow degrees since that era!

"This chair had stood firm when the thrones of kings were overturned!" thought Laurence. "Its oaken frame has proved stronger than many frames of government!"

More the thoughtful and imaginative boy might have mused; but now a large yellow cat, a great favorite with all the children, leaped in at the open window. Perceiving that Grandfather's chair was empty, and having often before experienced its comforts, puss laid herself quietly down upon the cushion. Laurence, Clara, Charley, and little Alice all laughed at the idea of such a successor to the worthies of old times.

"Pussy," said little Alice, putting out her hand, into which the cat laid a velvet paw, "you look very wise. Do tell us a story about GRANDFATHER'S CHAIR!"

THE END

Maynard's French Texts

A Series of French School Texts

This Series of French Texts is intended principally for beginners, although it will contain some volumes suitable for students who have attained some proficiency in reading. Each volume is carefully edited by an experienced teacher with notes or vocabulary or both, as the case may be. The type is large and clear and the volumes are tastefully bound in cloth.

Specimen copies sent by mail on receipt of the price

No. 1. La Belle au Bois Dormant. Le Chat Botté. *Elementary.* 24 pages text, 29 pages vocabulary. Cloth, price 20 cents.

No. 2. Méle-toi de ton Métier, by Mlle. L. Bruneau. *Elementary.* 18 pages text, 34 pages vocabulary. Cloth, price 20 cents.

No. 3. Huit Contes, by Mlle. Marie Minssen. *Elementary.* 25 pages text, 36 pages vocabulary. Cloth, price 20 cents.

No. 4. Historiettes. From the English. *Elementary.* 24 pages text, 35 pages vocabulary. Cloth, price 20 cents.

No. 5. Ce qu'on voit, by Mlle. E. de Pompéry. *Elementary.* 23 pages text, 36 pages vocabulary. Cloth, price 20 cents.

No. 6. Petites Histoires Enfantines, by Mlle. E. de Pompéry. *Elementary.* 22 pages text, 37 pages vocabulary. Cloth, price 20 cents.

No. 7. Petit Livre d'Instruction et de Divertissement. *Elementary.* 27 pages text, 37 pages vocabulary. Cloth, price 20 cents.

No. 8. Un Mariage d'Amour, by Ludovic Halévy. *Advanced.* 57 pages text, 5 pages appendix, 8 pages notes. Cloth, price 25 cents.

Maynard, Merrill, & Co. publish also the following standard French books:

La France. By A. de Rougemont, Professor of French at the Adelphi Academy, Brooklyn, N. Y., and in charge of the French course at Chautauqua. An entertaining and instructive reading book for French classes. Of special value for stimulating learners to speak. Used at Harvard College. Cloth, 188 pages, 75 cents.

"In seventeen short chapters we are told (in French) all about the soil, climate, population, industries, social classes, and principal cities of France; and in twenty-two chapters more the educational system, the language and universities, the literature, the arts, the sciences, religion, and domestic life of France are discussed."—*The Critic*, New York.

From Yale College: "I shall take every opportunity that may present itself to recommend its use."—Prof. W. D. WHITNEY.

From Amherst College: "It is almost the *ideal* book for which I have been looking."—Prof. W. L. MONTAGUE.

Anecdotes Nouvelles, Lectures faciles et amusantes et Récitations. Boards, 30 cents.

Elwall's English-French and French-English Dictionary. Compact, and beautifully printed. 18mo, 1300 pages, cloth, $2.00.

FRENCH COURSE BY PROF. JEAN GUSTAVE KEETELS

I. **A Child's Illustrated First Book in French.** 167 pages, 12mo, 75 cents.

The aim of this book is to teach children to speak French as they learn their mother tongue. It contains sufficient matter for a two years' course of instruction, and is intended for children from eight or ten years of age to twelve or fourteen years of age.

II. **An Elementary French Grammar.** 350 pages, 12mo. Price 95 cents.

This book is designed for students in high schools and academies who are beginning the study of French. Its purpose is to train them in the principles of French

Grammar, and to accustom them to speak French by oral instruction. The rules are stated in clear, correct, and concise language. The exercises are short, lively, and varied. It contains matter for a course of one or two years' instruction, and will prepare students to take up afterward the larger works, with the advantage of knowing much of the theoretical part, rendering their task in going through the course easier and surer.

A KEY TO THE ENGLISH EXERCISES IN THE ELEMENTARY FRENCH GRAMMAR. For Teachers only. 60 cents.

III. An Analytical and Practical French Grammar. 12mo, 554 pages, $1.50.

This work contains a complete system for learning to read, write, and speak the language. The practical part consists of oral exercises in the form of questions, which the teacher asks of the pupil, who is to answer them directly in French. This method insures fluency of utterance and correct pronunciation, and exercises the pupil in speaking French from the beginning.

The theoretical part of the work comprises the whole grammar in fifty-four lessons, accompanied by English exercises to be translated into French. The development of the different elements is in harmony with the logical construction of sentences.

Three lessons are devoted to Etymology, treating of words derived from the Latin and common to both French and English. This is an interesting part of the work.

Six lessons have been added, giving subjects for composition; containing some of the principal idioms in the language.

This work is the most complete text-book of French published in this country.

A KEY TO THE ENGLISH EXERCISES IN THE ANALYTICAL AND PRACTICAL FRENCH GRAMMAR. For Teachers only. 60 cents.

IV. A Collegiate Course in the French Language: Comprising a Complete Grammar in Two Parts. 550 pages, 12mo, attractively bound. Price for introduction, $1.50.

PART FIRST.—A Treatise on French Pronunciation; Rules of Gender; Etymology; Exercises for Translation; the Latin elements common to both French and English.

PART SECOND.—Syntax; a Collection of Idioms; Exercises for Translation, and Vocabulary.

This work, as its title indicates, is designed for colleges and collegiate institutions.

A KEY TO THE ENGLISH EXERCISES IN THE COLLEGIATE COURSE. For Teachers only. 60 cents.

V. An Analytical French Reader : with English Exercises for Translation and Oral Exercises for Practice in Speaking; Questions on Grammar, with References to the Author's several Grammars; Notes and Vocabulary. In Two Parts. PART FIRST : Selections of Fables, Anecdotes, and Short Stories. PART SECOND : Selections from the Best Modern Writers. 348 pages, 12mo. Price $1.25.

FRENCH PLAYS FOR GIRLS

BY VARIOUS AUTHORS

EDITED BY PROF. M. ÉMILE ROCHE

1. **Marguerite ; ou, La robe perdue.** Drame moral en un acte, mêlé de couplets. 25 cents.

2. **Les Ricochets.** Comédie en un acte, imitée de Picard avec couplets. 25 cents.

3. **Les Demoiselles d'Honneur; ou, Le lutin du soir.** Vaudeville en un acte. 25 cents.

4. **Les Demoiselles de Saint Cyr.** Petit drame moral en un acte. 25 cents.

5. **Un Reve.** Petit drame avec prologue et épilogue. 25 cents.

6. **Un Place à la Cour.** Comédie en un acte avec couplets. 25 cents.

MAYNARD, MERRILL, & CO., PUBLISHERS

43, 45, AND 47 EAST TENTH STREET, NEW YORK.

Maynard's German Texts
A Series of German School Texts
CAREFULLY EDITED BY SCHOLARS FAMILIAR WITH
THE NEEDS OF THE CLASS-ROOM

The distinguishing features of the Series are as follows:

The Texts are chosen only from modern German authors, in order to give the pupil specimens of the language as it is now written and spoken. The German prose style of the present differs so largely from that of the classical period of German literature, from which the books in the hands of pupils are generally taken, that the want of such texts must have been felt by every teacher of German.

Each volume contains, either in excerpt or *in extenso*, a piece of German prose which, whilst continuous enough to sustain interest, will not be too long to be finished in the work of a term or two.

The Series is composed of two progressive courses, the Elementary and the Advanced. Some of the volumes of the Elementary Course contain, in addition to the notes, a complete alphabetical vocabulary. In the remaining volumes of the Series difficulties of meaning, to which the ordinary school dictionaries offer no clew, are dealt with in the notes at the end of each book.

In order not to overburden the vocabularies with verbal forms occurring in the text, a list of the commoner strong verbs is added as an appendix to the volumes of the Elementary Course.

The modern German orthography is used throughout.

The same grammatical terminology is used in all the volumes of the Series.

The volumes are attractively bound in cloth, and the type is large and clear.

All the elementary numbers contain a valuable appendix on the strong and weak verbs.

Specimen copies sent by mail on receipt of the price.

No. 1. Ulysses und der Kyklop, from C. F. Becker's *Erzählungen aus der Alten Welt*. An especially easy number. *Elementary.* 21 pages text, 50 pages vocabulary. Cloth, 25 cents.

No. 2. Fritz auf dem Lande, by Hans Arnold. An easy number. *Elementary.* 29 pages text, 28 pages notes, 28 pages vocabulary, 4 pages appendix. Cloth, 25 cents.

No. 3. Bilder aus der Türkei, from Grube's *Geographische Characterbilder*. *Elementary.* 28 pages text, 25 pages notes, 43 pages vocabulary and appendix. Cloth, 25 cents.

No. 4. Weihnachten bei Leberecht Hünchen, by Heinrich Seidel. *Elementary.* 26 pages text, 36 pages notes, 34 pages vocabulary and appendix. Cloth, 25 cents.

No. 5. Die Wandelnde Glocke, from *Der Lahrer Hinkende Bote*, by Wilhelm Fischer. *Elementary.* 33 pages text, 24 pages notes, 38 pages vocabulary and appendix. Cloth, 25 cents.

No. 6. Der Besuch im Carcer, Humoreske, by Ernst Eckstein. *Elementary.* 31 pages text, 23 pages notes, 30 pages vocabulary and appendix. Cloth, 25 cents.

No. 7. Episodes from **Andreas Hofer**, by Otto Hoffman. *Elementary.* 78 pages text, 18 pages notes. Cloth, 25 cents.

No. 8. Die Werke der Barmherzigkeit, by W. H. Riehl. *Elementary.* 60 pages text, 34 pages notes. Cloth, 25 cents.

No. 9. Harold, Trauerspiel in fünf Akten, by Ernst von Wildenbruch. *Advanced.* 4 pages introduction, 115 pages text, 18 pages notes. Cloth, 40 cents.

No. 10. Kolberg, Historisches Schauspiel in fünf Akten, by Paul Heyse. *Advanced.* 112 pages text, 25 pages notes. Cloth, 40 cents.

No. 11. Robert Blake (ein Seestück) und **Cromwell**, zwei ausgewählte Aufsätze, by Reinhold Pauli. *Advanced.* 2 pages preface, 93 pages text, 53 pages notes. Cloth, 40 cents.

No. 12. Das deutsche Ordensland Preussen, by H. von Treitschke. *Advanced.* With map, 77 pages text, 62 pages notes. Cloth, 40 cents.

No. 13. Meister Martin Hildebrand, by W. H. Riehl. *Advanced.* An easy volume. 3 pages introduction, 53 pages text, 35 pages notes. Cloth, 40 cents.

No. 14. Die Lehrjahre eines Humanisten, by W. H. Riehl. *Advanced.* 55 pages text, 47 pages notes. Cloth, 40 cents.

No. 15. Aus dem Jahrhundert des Grossen Krieges, by Gustav Freytag. *Advanced.* 28 pages introduction, 85 pages text, 41 pages notes. Cloth, 40 cents.

Goethe's Italienische Reise. (*Selected Letters.*) With introduction, 16 pages, map, text, 98 pages, notes, 48 pages. Edited by H. S. BERESFORD-WEBB, *Examiner in German (Prelim.) to the University of Glasgow.* Cloth, 50 cents.

This selection does not profess to cover entirely new ground, as only a limited portion of the letters is available for educational purposes, the remainder being beyond the reach of ordinary students ; but while a few passages have been omitted which the editor deemed unsuitable or not sufficiently interesting, a large number have been added which have not appeared in previous selections.

TWO GERMAN READERS

Easy Readings in German on Familiar Subjects.

Consisting of 100 Easy German Stories, 89 pages, with Exercises for re-translation, 31 pages, and English-German and German-English vocabularies, 79 pages. By A. R. LECHNER, Senior Master of Modern Languages, Modern School, Bedford, England. Cloth, 50 cents.

Most of the pieces here have been adapted from English sources, so that the probable acquaintance of most young people with the subjects will render them more interesting, and facilitate their translation into English. The language used throughout is of the simplest kind, and the author has endeavored to use only such words as occur in daily life. The same words are frequently repeated with the view of impressing them on the memory.

Beginner's German Translation Book.

Consisting of German Stories and Anecdotes, 64 pages, with Exercises for re-translation, 50 pages, notes, 18 pages, and German-English and English-German vocabularies, 99 pages. By H. S. BERESFORD-WEBB, *Examiner in German (Prelim.) to the University of Glasgow.* Cloth, 50 cents.

The object of this book is, first, to provide a Reading Book for beginners,—and for this purpose the passages in Part I. (pp. 1-9) have been adapted and arranged in such a manner as to introduce the reader gradually to the various forms and constructions of the language,—and secondly, to train the learner to utilize his stock of knowledge, acquired in translating from the German, by reproducing sentences similar to those he has read ; in other words, to encourage imitation and adaptation. A learner hears or reads a construction or phrase, understands it, but is unable, from want of practice or confidence, to use it himself. Very often this difficulty arises from the necessity of changing slightly the construction, and adapting it to what he is desirous of saying. The Exercises have therefore been compiled with a view to give constant practice in the development of this faculty, and though, of course, this is not all that is required when learning a language, it will go a long way towards overcoming the difficulties which present themselves to the intelligent learner.

Maynard, Merrill, & Co. publish also the following standard German books:

Neuer Leitfaden.

By EDWIN F. BACON, Ph.B., Professor of Modern Languages at the Oneonta State Normal School. This book meets a real want by its skillful employment of the natural or conversational method without the sacrifice of the grammatical thoroughness essential to a complete knowledge of the language. It is divided into two parts: the first a conversation grammar arranged in concise single-page lessons, remarkably convenient for reference ; the second a choice, collection of short stories, dialogues, and songs with music, to which is added a complete German-English vocabulary.

It is believed that this book, being free from all the objections so often urged against the natural method, will contribute greatly to the popularity and spread of that method. It teaches the grammar ; but it is grammar by practice, not by rule. The twelve introductory lessons are a rare example of ingenuity in the conversational presentation of the elements of the language, and, in the hands of a skillful teacher, are calculated to prepare for rapid and intelligent progress through the admirable single-page lessons that follow. These lessons contain a clear outline, the *essentials,* of the grammar without that minuteness of detail which renders so many text-books in language too bulky for ordinary use or convenient reference. Cloth, $1.25.

Kostyak and Ader's Deutschland und die Deutschen.

The land where German is spoken and the people who speak it. An excellent German reader. Cloth, 75 cents.

Neue Anekdoten: Leichte und heitere Stücke.

A collection of amusing and instructive anecdotes which furnish excellent material for reading and conversation. Boards, 40 cents.

MAYNARD, MERRILL, & CO., PUBLISHERS,

43, 45, AND 47 EAST TENTH STREET, NEW YORK.

ENGLISH CLASSIC SERIES—CONTINUED.

The Antigone of Sophocles. English Version by Thos. Francklin, D.D.
Elizabeth Barrett Browning. (Selected Poems.)
Robert Browning. (Selected Poems.)
Addison's Spectator. (Selec'ns.)
Scenes from George Eliot's Adam Bede.
Matthew Arnold's Culture and Anarchy.
DeQuincey's Joan of Arc.
Carlyle's Essay on Burns.
Byron's Childe Harold's Pilgrimage.
Poe's Raven, and other Poems.
& 74 Macaulay's Lord Clive. (Double Number.)
Webster's Reply to Hayne.
& 77 Macaulay's Lays of Ancient Rome. (Double Number.)
American Patriotic Selections: Declaration of Independence, Washington's Farewell Address, Lincoln's Gettysburg Speech, etc.
& 80 Scott's Lady of the Lake. (Condensed.)
& 82 Scott's Marmion. (Condensed.)
& 84 Pope's Essay on Man.
Shelley's Skylark, Adonais, and other Poems.
Dickens's Cricket on the Hearth.
Spencer's Philosophy of Style.
Lamb's Essays of Elia.
Cowper's Task, Book II.
Wordsworth's Selected Poems.
Tennyson's The Holy Grail, and Sir Galahad.
Addison's Cato.
Irving's Westminster Abbey, and Christmas Sketches.
& 95 Macaulay's Earl of Chatham. Second Essay.
Early English Ballads.
Skelton, Wyatt, and Surrey. (Selected Poems.)
Edwin Arnold. (Selected Poems.)
Caxton and Daniel. (Selections.)
0 Fuller and Hooker. (Selections.)
1 Marlowe's Jew of Malta. (Condensed.)
2-103 Macaulay's Essay on Milton.
4-105 Macaulay's Essay on Addison.
5 Macaulay's Essay on Boswell's Johnson.

107 Mandeville's Travels and Wycliffe's Bible. (Selections.)
108-109 Macaulay's Essay on Frederick the Great.
110-111 Milton's Samson Agonistes.
112-113-114 Franklin's Autobiography.
115-116 Herodotus's Stories of Crœsus, Cyrus, and Babylon.
117 Irving's Alhambra.
118 Burke's Present Discontents.
119 Burke's Speech on Conciliation with American Colonies.
120 Macaulay's Essay on Byron.
121-122 Motley's Peter the Great.
123 Emerson's American Scholar.
124 Arnold's Sohrab and Rustum.
125-126 Longfellow's Evangeline.
127 Andersen's Danish Fairy Tales. (Selected.)
128 Tennyson's The Coming of Arthur, and The Passing of Arthur.
129 Lowell's The Vision of Sir Launfal, and other Poems.
130 Whittier's Songs of Labor, and other Poems.
131 Words of Abraham Lincoln.
132 Grimm's German Fairy Tales. (Selected.)
133 Æsop's Fables. (Selected.)
134 Arabian Nights. Aladdin, or the Wonderful Lamp.
135-36 The Psalter.
137-38 Scott's Ivanhoe. (Condensed.)
139-40 Scott's Kenilworth. (Condensed.)
141-42 Scott's The Talisman. (Condensed.)
143 Gods and Heroes of the North.
144-45 Pope's Iliad of Homer. (Selections from Books I.-VIII.)
146 Four Mediæval Chroniclers.
147 Dante's Inferno. (Condensed.)
148-49 The Book of Job. (Revised Version.)
150 Bow-Wow and Mew-Mew. By Georgiana M. Craik.
151 The Nürnberg Stove. By Ouida.
152 Hayne's Speech. To which Webster replied.
153 Alice's Adventures in Wonderland. (Condensed.) By Lewis Carroll.
154-155 Defoe's Journal of the Plague. (Condensed.)
156-157 More's Utopia. (Condensed.)

ADDITIONAL NUMBERS ON NEXT PAGE.

ENGLISH CLASSIC SERIES—CONTINUED.

158-159 **Lamb's Essays.** (Selections.)
160-161 **Burke's Reflections on the French Revolution.**
162-163 **Macaulay's History of England, Chapter I.** *Complete.*
164-165-166 **Prescott's Conquest of Mexico.** (Condensed.)
167 **Longfellow's Voices of the Night, and other poems.**
168 **Hawthorne's Wonder Book. Selected Tales.**
169 **DeQuincey's Flight of a Tartar Tribe.** Complete.
170-171-172 **George Eliot's Silas Marner.** Complete.
173 **Ruskin's King of the Golden River, and Dame Wiggins of Lee and her Seven Wonderful Cats.**
174-175 **Irving's Tales of a Traveler.**
176 **Ruskin's Of Kings' Treasuries.** First half of *Sesame and Lilies.* Complete.
177 **Ruskin's Of Queens' Gardens.** Second half of *Sesame and Lilies.* Complete.
178 **Macaulay's Life of Johnson.**
179-180 **Defoe's Robinson Crusoe.**
181-182-183 **Wykes's Shakespeare Reader.**
184 **Hawthorne's Grandfather's Chair.** Part I. Complete.

New numbers will be added from time to time.

Single numbers, 32 to 96 pages; mailing price, 12 cents per copy. Double numbers, 75 to 158 pages; mailing price, 24 cents per copy.

SPECIAL NUMBERS.

Milton's Paradise Lost. Book I. With portrait and biographical sketch of Milton, and full introductory and explanatory notes. Bound in Boards. *Mailing price, 30 cents.*
Milton's Paradise Lost. Books I. and II. With portrait and biographical sketch of Milton, and full introductory and explanatory notes. Boards. *Mailing price, 40 cents.*
Chaucer's The Canterbury Tales. The Prologue. With portrait and biographical sketch of the author, introductory and explanatory notes, brief history of English language to time of Chaucer, and glossary. Bound in boards. *Mailing price, 35 cents.*
Chaucer's The Squieres Tale. With portrait and biographical sketch of author, glossary, and full explanatory notes Boards. *Mailing price, 35 cents.*
Chaucer's The Knightes Tale. With portrait and biographical sketch of author, glossary, and full explanatory notes. Boards. *Mailing price, 40 cents.*
Goldsmith's She Stoops to Conquer. With biographical sketch of author, and full explanatory notes. Boards. *Mailing price, 30 cents.*
Homer's Iliad. Books I. and VI. Metrical translation by GEORGE HOWLAND. With introduction and notes. *Mailing price, 25 cents.*
Homer's Odyssey. Books I., V., IX., and X. Metrical translation by GEORGE HOWLAND. With introduction and notes. *Mailing price, 25 cents.*
Horace's The Art of Poetry. Translated in verse by GEORGE HOWLAND. *Mailing price, 25 cents.*
The Story of the German Iliad, with Related Stories. With a full glossary and review of the Influence of the Nibelungen Lied through Richard Wagner. By MARY E. BURT. Illustrated. 128 pages, 12mo, cloth. *Mailing price, 50 cents.*

Special Prices to Teachers.

FULL DESCRIPTIVE CATALOGUE SENT ON APPLICATION.